Hart Crane's *The Bridge*

Frontispiece. The Bridge and Lower Manhattan, 1934.

Hart Crane's *The Bridge*

AN ANNOTATED EDITION
Edited by Lawrence Kramer

Fordham University Press | New York 2011

Library of Congress Cataloging-in-Publication Data
Crane, Hart, 1899–1932.
   [Bridge]
   Hart Crane's The bridge : an annotated edition /
edited by Lawrence Kramer. — 1st ed.
      p.   cm.
   Includes bibliographical references.
   ISBN 978-0-8232-3307-6 (cloth : alk. paper)
   I. Kramer, Lawrence, 1946– II. Title.
   PS35.05R272B7 2011
   811'.52—dc22
2011000287

Printed in the United States of America
13   5 4 3 2
First edition

CONTENTS

ILLUSTRATIONS

ACKNOWLEDGMENTS

The Editorial Assistants

Editorial assistants are listed after the titles of the sections on which they worked.

To Brooklyn Bridge	Shoghig Halajian
Ave Maria	Laura Hydak
The Harbor Dawn	Tasha Kohl
Van Winkle	Virginia Dare Holmes
The River	Allison Miller
The Dance	Jill Neziri
Indiana	Lea Flis
Cutty Sark	Jill Neziri, Lea Flis, Allison Miller
Cape Hatteras	Matt Leporati, Melissa Goldstein, Katya Kulik, Kimberly Durkota
Southern Cross	Matt Leporati
National Winter Garden	Katya Kulik
Virginia	Melissa Goldstein
Quaker Hill	Karina Everett
The Tunnel	Alison Maher
Atlantis	Lou Scerra

SOURCES

The text of *The Bridge* in this edition follows Crane's corrected proofs to the second edition, published in New York by Liveright in 1930; Crane preferred this text to the first edition, published in Paris by Black Sun Press in the same year. The corrected Liveright text is the one used by *The Complete Poems of Hart Crane: A Centennial Edition*, edited by Marc Simon (New York: Liveright, 1986).

Crane's letters are from *The Letters of Hart Crane: 1916–1932*, edited by Brom Weber (Berkeley: University of California Press, 1965).

To avoid annotating the annotation, the notes in this edition acknowledge specific scholarly debts informally. But three sources require full acknowledgment here. For information on the burlesque scene in the 1920s: Gordon A. Tapper, *The Machine That Sings: Modernism, Hart Crane, and the Culture of the Body* (New York: Routledge, 2006). For popular song texts of the day: John Irwin, "Hart Crane's *The Bridge II*," *Raritan* 9 (2006): 99–113, and Susan Jenkins Brown, *Robber Rocks: Letters and Memories of Hart Crane* (Middletown, CT: Wesleyan University Press, 1969).

ANNOTATING *The Bridge*

Lawrence Kramer

Hart Crane's long poem *The Bridge* has steadily grown in stature since it was published in 1930. At first branded a noble failure by a few influential critics—a charge that became conventional wisdom—this panoramic work is now widely regarded as one of the finest achievements of twentieth-century American poetry. Like Walt Whitman's *Leaves of Grass*, with which it maintains a running dialogue, *The Bridge* constitutes an epochal statement about American life and character. Like Whitman's major poems, *The Bridge* is epic in scope and rhapsodic in language. Like Whitman's "Song of Myself" and "Passage to India," it unites mythology and modernity as a means of coming to terms with the promises, both kept and broken, of American experience.

But *The Bridge* is also a hugely difficult work. Although the poem is widely loved among readers of poetry, appreciation of it seems to rest primarily on its many scattered passages of undeniable but self-sufficient lyrical brilliance. These have proven capable, like the cables of a suspension bridge, of holding up a weight much greater than their own. Nonetheless, the plain fact is that the general conception of *The Bridge*, much less the detailed execution of it, remains beyond the reach of most readers. Obscure and indirect allusions abound, some of them at surprisingly fine levels of detail; elaborate compound metaphors conflate disparate sources and often make it very difficult to say what, if anything, is "going on" in the text. The poem is replete with topical and geographical references that demand explication as well as identification. Many passages are simply incomprehensible without special knowledge, often special knowledge of a sort that is not readily available even today, when Google and Wikipedia are only a click away.

It is impossible, for example, to understand the first large section, "Ave Maria," without detailed knowledge of Columbus's journey home from his first voyage to the Americas, or to understand the pivotal "Cutty Sark" section without similarly detailed knowledge of the history of clipper ships and their trade. "Cape Hatteras" plunges the reader deep into the history of aviation—and also into the poetry of Walt Whitman. "The Dance" involves a farrago of anthropological and historical information and misinformation about both Native American and Mesoamerican cultures and world religions.

Although the critical literature on *The Bridge* does furnish bits and pieces of the pertinent information for these sections and others, pulling all of the data together demands considerable effort. Until now there has been no single source to which a reader can go for help. There has been no convenient guide to the poem's labyrinthine complexities and its dense network of allusions—the "thousands of strands" that, Crane boasted "had to be sorted out, researched, and interwoven" to compose the work (letter to Otto Kahn, September 12, 1927). Crane would discern the same interweaving of strands in the Brooklyn Bridge itself, whose suspension cables form perhaps the poem's primary image and source of images. Woven strands represent both what *The Bridge* seeks to embody and how it seeks to be read.

The opportunity to supply a guide to reading it arose a few years ago in the English Department of Fordham University, when I taught a graduate seminar entitled Research Methods. The topic of the course was how to answer a deceptively simple question: What do I have to know to make sense of this—that is, of any—text? The twelve students in the class tackled the question primarily by writing annotation to the poetry of Hart Crane. Under my supervision they glossed lines, supplied references, found parallels, unearthed contexts, detected echoes of earlier poetry and literary prose, tracked down allusions both overt and covert and explained both kinds, untangled syntax, teased apart compound metaphors, and so on. They then drafted annotated texts, which, after critique and review, they proceeded to revise.

The edition you now have in hand synthesizes their work, winnows it, adds to it, and develops it further. Although most of the language and all of the final decisions about what to gloss and what to let stand are mine, as are the inevitable mistakes, this edition would not have been possible without the students' research. The formal Acknowledgments accordingly credits, with sincere thanks, all those who worked on the poem's various sections as assistant editors.

The editorial work was simplified by the happy fact that there are no significant textual problems with *The Bridge*. There are a small number of minor textual variants, a list of which is available in the Liveright Centennial Edition, edited by Marc Simon. But these are of limited interest even to scholars; they have virtually no substantive impact on the meaning of the poem. For general readers, they are curiosities at best. With *The Bridge* we know without question what to read. The question is how to read it.

The purpose of this volume is not to answer that question but to make it more readily askable. The annotation to the text is intended not to fix or impose a reading but to help readers compose their own. Nonetheless, the selection of what to annotate and how to annotate it inevitably implies a certain understanding, an interpretive horizon that bounds the text. This boundary is neither unfortunate nor a mere side effect; the text would not be intelligible at all without it. But with a text as elusive as *The Bridge*, the interweaving—to adopt Crane's metaphor—of glossing and interpreting is especially acute. It is best to be open about this necessary entanglement and to sketch out a baseline of understanding that readers are free either to follow, to circumvent, or a little of both.

The Bridge is commonly thought of as a compact epic, although, unlike most of its precursors in the genre, it has no single hero and records no single narrative. Like many modernist texts, it is a kind of collage. It assembles itself from micro-narratives about actions and desires widely separated in both geography and history. It recounts those narratives in poetic forms ranging from strict rhymed quatrains to virtual delirium (sometimes both at once). It stuffs itself with lore both common (in the 1920s) and arcane, and what it cannot find it is happy to invent.

Nonetheless, the poem does concentrate on a trio of traditional epic themes, which it seeks to reinterpret in relation to modern life. First, there is the voyage or journey, which forms the fundamental action in virtually all of the poem's thirteen sections. *The Bridge* begins and ends in the New York harbor of its namesake, but in between it wanders across the continent in a kind of prophetic *flanerie*—by air, by water, by rail, on foot, on horseback, on the road. Spanning or traversing is the poem's fundamental metaphor; *The Bridge* spans the continent as the Bridge spans the East River.

Second, there is the relationship between past and present, the basic armature of history. The poem represents this not as an irreversible sequence but as a series of wave motions. History takes shape as a continuous overlapping of ripples produced by actions and desires echoing and repeating each other across time, sometimes divided by years, sometimes by centuries.

Finally, there is the possibility of understanding history as a purposive, even redemptory process, in particular, one destined to find its consummation in the New World. The idea of redemption implies a prior experience of fall or decline. It is the avowed aim of *The Bridge* to formulate a New World myth, an American myth, that will both imagine and contribute to a world-historical passage from decline to regeneration. The material form of that myth is the Brooklyn Bridge, apostrophes to which frame the work. The dynamic form is the rediscovery, within the socially and technologically disrupted world of modernity, of the unfulfilled but perhaps still fulfillable promises of a heroic or utopian past.

Crane's descriptions of the debased features of the present are as unsparing as T. S. Eliot's in *The Waste Land*, to which *The Bridge* forms a direct counterstatement. But Crane's overarching intent is visionary, not denunciatory; his real teacher is not Eliot but Whitman, a lineage the poem explicitly dramatizes in "Cape Hatteras." This orientation may in part explain why *The Bridge*—composed between 1926 and 1930 and continually revised—ultimately takes no particular notice of the Great Depression, whose force Crane seems willfully to have underestimated, even though it ruined his own financial situation and may have contributed to his suicide. The poem is driven by an irrepressible utopianism, even though its utopian episodes are brief, scattered flashes across a world by turns mundane, shabby, violent, and agonizing.

In the persistence of the past Crane finds a teleology, or better, perhaps, an eschatology (albeit a purely secular one), which can be ignored or betrayed but not destroyed. "What I am after," he wrote, "is an . . . organic panorama, showing the continuous and living evidence of the past in the inmost vital substance of the present" (letter to Otto Kahn, September 12, 1927). The Brooklyn Bridge realizes this possibility by virtue of its dual status as a technological marvel (for twenty years after its completion in 1883 it was the longest suspension bridge in the world) and an aesthetic achievement.

Crane was not alone in regarding the Bridge as "the most superb and original example of American architecture yet hinted at" or in being moved by "the marvelous feeling the webbed cables give (as one advances) of a simultaneous forward and upward motion" of mythic proportions (letter to Yvor Winters, April 29, 1927). He knew the hectic and heroic paintings of the Bridge by the modernist artist Joseph Stella, as well as the photographs of it by Walker Evans, who became a friend; photographs by Evans eventually served as illustrations to the first (Black Sun) edition of *The Bridge*, although Crane's first thought had been to use reproductions of paintings by Stella. Like Crane, Stella saw the Bridge as redemptive in its sublimity. Although he was more ambivalent about the links of the "metallic apparition" to "the underground tumult of the trains in perpetual motion" and "the strange moanings of appeal from tug boats"—both images found in Crane—the Bridge still drew Stella forward and upward "as if on the threshold of a new religion or in the presence of a new divinity" (Stella, "The Brooklyn Bridge: A Page of My Life"; 1928). Crane built his poem around the same metaphor: "Terrific threshold of the prophet's pledge!"

Modernity could and would do its worst, and Crane, whose poem says as much, in the end would not survive its dislocations. But the poem permanently enshrines the utopian promise of American history in the "curveship" of the great Bridge, whose architecture is also the poem's architecture. Invoked twice, as if once for each of its support towers, the Bridge anchors the span of the whole with twin odes steeped in the rhetoric of the sublime: the solemn "To Brooklyn Bridge" that begins *The Bridge* and the delirious "Atlantis" that ends it.

The Bridge, the poem, the continent, the years—*The Bridge* aspires to do more than simply represent or symbolize its nested spans. Crane's involvement with Stella and Evans is symptomatic. The poem's metaphorically dense, rhetorically and rhythmically marked verse aims to make its spans *appear* in quasi-hallucinatory form. Reading becomes panoramic seeing; the poem rolls by like a transcendental newsreel. The impression of architectural grandeur, the concentrated form of the wide expanses traversed between "To Brooklyn Bridge" and "Atlantis," is fundamental to both framing segments. At the midpoint of "Atlantis" Crane marks the apogee of this sublime visuality when he ceremoniously christens the Bridge "Tall Vision-of-the Voyage." Accordingly, this edition supplements its annotation with a series of photographs, drawn from the collection of the Library of Congress, depicting the poem's key New York landmarks—the Bridge itself, South Street Seaport, Columbus Circle, Broadway, the Woolworth Building—as they looked in the early years of the twentieth century.

But the span of *The Bridge* is more than visual. The framing poems also invoke the idea of a sublime music, a modern and secular version of the traditional music of the spheres. The sound of that music is meant to become audible in the long span of a verse that resonates like the "bound cable strands" of the Bridge recalled in the first stanza of "Atlantis":

> Taut miles of shuttling moonlight syncopate
> The whispered rush, telepathy of wires.
> Up the index of night, granite and steel—
> Transparent meshes—fleckless the gleaming staves—
> Sibylline voices flicker, waveringly stream
> As if a god were issue of the strings.

One dimension of the "telepathy of wires" is the multitude of echoes whose "whispered rush" sounds throughout the text across both time and space— not, as in Eliot's *The Waste Land*, as the debris of a ruined civilization, but as the unfinished resonance of the making of the New World. The Sibylline voices of this music are obscure by definition, and at one level the experience of reading *The Bridge* is meant to resist glosses and explanations; the poem is both a construction fit for an age of granite and steel and an inducement to oracular reverie. But at another level, equally explicit, the poem is about rewriting history in the form of myth. That is a project that requires footnotes; this annotated edition is meant to provide them.

THE BRIDGE

From going to and fro in the earth,
And from walking up and down in it.

—The Book of Job

1. The Bridge at Night, ca. 1903.

EPIGRAPH: From Job 1:6–7: "There was a day when the sons of God came to present themselves before the Lord, and Satan came also among them. . . . And the Lord said unto Satan, 'From whence comest thou?'" The epigraph is Satan's answer; it introduces the motif of wandering that pervades *The Bridge*. Perhaps more importantly, by quoting Satan as a guide it links visionary poetics with secular energy in the manner of William Blake's *The Marriage of Heaven and Hell*, where "the Devil or Satan" represents desire in eternal constructive opposition to reason.

TO BROOKLYN BRIDGE

How many dawns, chill from his rippling rest
⎿ The seagull's wings shall dip and pivot him,[1]
Shedding white rings of tumult, building high
Over the chained bay waters Liberty—[2]

TO BROOKLYN BRIDGE: In his correspondence Crane regularly referred to this poem as the Dedication to *The Bridge*. The second edition prints it in italics; the present edition reverts to Roman type to facilitate ease of movement between the text and the annotation.

1. The image of the seagull immediately connects Crane's poetic voice with those of his two primary interlocutors in *The Bridge*, Walt Whitman and T. S. Eliot. Soaring and dipping gulls preside over New York harbor in Whitman's "Crossing Brooklyn Ferry," which "To Brooklyn Bridge" takes as a model and silent preamble. Whitman's poem is also set near dawn ("the sun there half an hour high"). Its celebration of the ferry that the Bridge would replace takes the circling seagull as a primary image, connoting both a soaring leap and an act of connection—the two motions of the Bridge evoked in "To Brooklyn Bridge":

> I too many and many a time cross'd the river of old,
> Watched the Twelfth-month sea-gulls, saw them high in the air
>   floating with motionless wings, oscillating their bodies,
> Saw how the glistening yellow lit up parts of their bodies and left
>   the rest in strong shadow,
> Saw the slow-wheeling circles and the gradual edging toward the south,
> Saw the reflection of the summer sky in the water. (ll. 27–31)

The tumult of the gull hovers more darkly over "Death by Water," the fourth section of Eliot's *The Waste Land*, which begins with the image of the drowned Phoenician sailor: "Phlebas the Phoenician, a fortnight dead. / Forgot the cry of gulls, and the deep sea swell, / And the profit and the loss." The contrary allusions articulate contrary representations of the city, both of which *The Bridge* seeks to supplant. Unlike Eliot's London, the "Unreal City" merged with the world of the dead, Crane's Manhattan is not an exhausted dystopia. But unlike Whitman's utopian Manhattan, it is nonetheless a fallen city, very much a version of the unregenerate City of Man envisioned by St. Augustine (a figure also invoked in *The Waste Land*), but nonetheless a city in which the possibility of redemption continually breaks through in glimpses and glimmers. The gull here may also be a latter-day version of the albatross in Baudelaire's poem of the same name: a creature symbolic of the poet, who is free and inspired when on the wing but clumsy and even absurd when forced to walk to and fro.

2. The gull has been resting on the waters; his wings "dip and pivot him" as he takes flight and produce white-flecked circular ripples ("white rings of tumult") on the surface that anticipate the "inviolate curve" of his ascent. "Liberty" is the Statue of Liberty, visible from the Brooklyn side of the Bridge; the gull "builds," or more properly rebuilds, the statue above the waters, raising itself aloft as if an extension of the statue's torch. The bay waters may be "chained" because not all of the would-be immigrants who, seeking liberty, passed the statue en route to the processing center on Ellis Island were permitted to enter the country, or the phrase might refer more literally to the cordage associated with shipping and other industry.

Then, with inviolate curve, forsake our eyes   5
As apparitional as sails that cross
Some page of figures to be filed away;
—Till elevators drop us from our day . . .

I think of cinemas, panoramic sleights   9
With multitudes bent toward some flashing scene
Never disclosed, but hastened to again,
Foretold to other eyes on the same screen; [3]

And Thee, across the harbor, silver-paced   13
As though the sun took step of thee, yet left
Some motion ever unspent in thy stride,—
Implicitly thy freedom staying thee![4]

Out of some subway scuttle, cell or loft   17
A bedlamite speeds to thy parapets,[5]

3. The crowd at the movies may represent a debased version of the multitudes invoked by Whitman in "Crossing Brooklyn Ferry," where the poet's perception of the harbor scene foretells a bridging of the gap between distant generations:

> Others will enter the gates of the ferry and cross from shore to shore,
> Others will watch the run of the flood-tide,
> Others will see the shipping of Manhattan north and west, and the
>   heights of Brooklyn to the south and east,
> Others will see the islands large and small;
> Fifty years hence, others will see them as they cross. (ll. 13–17)

4. The imagery in this stanza may be taken to represent the Bridge as a latter-day Jacob's ladder on which the sun itself "takes step" and, like the gulls, travels between earth and heaven; the biblical reference is to Genesis 28:11–12: "And he lighted upon a certain place, and tarried there all night, because the sun was set. . . . And he dreamed, and behold a ladder set up on the earth, and the top of it reached to heaven: and behold the angels of God ascending and descending on it." The epithet "silver-paced" is difficult to gloss. The sun's traditional color is, of course, gold, whereas silver is the moon's; perhaps the point is that the Bridge's steel suspension cables appear in celestial silver as the sunlight that passes through them "takes step" from the Bridge's curvature.

5. Crane's use of the archaic "bedlamite" for "lunatic," a usage derived from the eighteenth-century London asylum St. Mary's of Bethlehem ("Bedlam") connects the conditions of industrial modernity (exemplified here by the "scuttle"—both coal bucket and roof hatch—of the subway stairwell and in the next stanza by violent construction work and turning derricks) with traditional images of isolation (the cell or loft, sites proper to hermits and impoverished poets) and urban disorder, symptoms of unregenerate life in the City of Man. At the same time, the term glosses life in the modern city as itself a "bedlam" in the latter-day sense of an overwhelming scene of noisy confusion (hence the epithet "shrill" transferred to the bedlamite's shirt, which balloons in the wind but cannot reverse his fall).

Tilting there momently, shrill shirt ballooning,
A jest falls from the speechless caravan.[6]

Down Wall,[7] from girder into street noon leaks,   21
A rip-tooth of the sky's acetylene;[8]
All afternoon the cloud-flown derricks turn . . .[9]
Thy cables breathe the North Atlantic still.

And obscure as that heaven of the Jews,[10]   25
Thy guerdon . . . Accolade thou dost bestow
Of anonymity time cannot raise:
Vibrant reprieve and pardon thou dost show.

O harp and altar, of the fury fused,   29
(How could mere toil align thy choiring strings!) [11]

6. The bedlamite's suicide becomes a form of mock or inverted nobility, also of archaic cast; the place from which, reversing the arc of the gull, the madman plunges is a castle's parapet, and his teetering there takes the form of a "tilting," meaning not only a leaning and a going out of alignment but also a jousting. The bedlamite thus becomes the victim of a cosmic joke, a "jest," with a pun on "gest," heroic deed. The "speechless caravan" (presumably of passing cars oblivious to the bedlamite's fate) may faintly suggest the image of the Dance of Death.

7. Wall Street, into whose narrow span the noon light leaks through the girders of skyscrapers under construction.

8. "Rip-tooth" presumably refers to a ripsaw, but the apposition between "rip-tooth" and "noon" suggests that the noon falls into the street like an extracted tooth. The image becomes less bizarre in connection with the theme of poetic vocation, already intimated by the gull and the bedlamite and soon to be invoked directly in the "prophet's pledge, / Prayer of pariah, and the lover's cry." As a prefatory poem, "To Brooklyn Bridge" is charged with finding its way to the speaker's Muse, which the Bridge will unequivocally become in the final stanza.

9. The vertical lines of Crane's derricks recall the "numberless masts of ships" in Whitman's New York harbor. Like "Crossing Brooklyn Ferry," though without its assured sense of enchantment, "To Brooklyn Bridge" seeks to sublimate the play of technology and commerce (and Eliot's "the profit and the loss") on the river; compare Whitman: "Come on, ships from the lower bay! . . . / Burn high your fires, foundry chimneys! cast black shadows at nightfall! cast red and yellow light over the tops of houses!" (ll. 117, 119).

10. Sheol, the Old Testament parallel to the classical Hades. The "heaven of the Jews" is "obscure" in part because it is literally dark, located in an abyss (the term *Sheol* is usually taken to mean "pit" or "abyss") but also because it is ambiguous. Both the righteous and unrighteous dead dwell there; their existence resembles their mortal life but only in etiolated form, like that of the shadows in Hades; Sheol is at once a place of torment and a place of rest. After the advent of Christianity, Sheol was understood by some to be the site where the dead awaited resurrection.

11. The Bridge fuses the harp and altar in the joining of its cable strands with the triumph of engineering that created its sun-inspiring "stride" across the river. This fusion becomes the symbol, but also an advance realization, of a reconciliation of body and spirit, song and sacrifice, aesthetics and religion. But at the same time this fusion is impossible, or at least incredible: "How can mere toil align [tune, turn into a harmonious scale] thy choiring strings?" The altar is both pagan and Christian, just as the harp alludes to both the lyres of

Terrific threshold of the prophet's pledge,
Prayer of pariah, and the lover's cry,—[12]

Again the traffic lights that skim thy swift   33
Unfractioned idiom, immaculate sigh of stars,
Beading thy path—condense eternity: [13]
And we have seen night lifted in thine arms.[14]

Under thy shadow by the piers I waited;   37
Only in darkness is thy shadow clear.[15]

Apollo and Orpheus and the harp of David the Psalmist. The Bridge as harp is also a gigantic Aeolian harp, a stringed instrument popular in the early nineteenth century that made random sounds as its strings were swept by the wind. Both Wordsworth (in *The Prelude*) and Coleridge (in "The Aeolian Harp") took the wind harp to be an image of the poetic imagination.

12. Prophet, pariah, and lover are all roles assumed explicitly by Crane during the course of *The Bridge* (e.g., in "Atlantis," "The Tunnel," and "The Harbor Dawn"), but the allusion here may be personal as well; the area under Brooklyn Bridge was a favorite cruising ground for homosexuals, Crane among them, who would have qualified then as both pariahs and lovers.

13. The term *immaculate* suggests a state free from sin, especially in association with the rosary implied in the image of "beading thy path"; the starry traffic lights "condense eternity" because the actual stars, in traditional cosmology, bead the canopy of the heavens. The stars are said to "sigh" in reference to the music of the spheres, the harmonious sound, usually inaudible to mortals, thought to be made by the celestial bodies as they rotate in space. The conception originates in classical Greece (with Pythagoras, whose cosmic music will also hover allusively behind "Atlantis") but was subsequently adopted by Christian Europe. At the same time, the cosmic harmony, thus brought to earth, appears as the model for an "unfractioned" (intact, integral) poetic idiom, the very idiom in which *The Bridge* seeks to "sing." The sound (or here, the synesthetically transferred sight) of this harmony suggests that the "reprieve and pardon" referred to in l. 28 is "vibrant" in the literal sense that it is transmitted via the vibrations of the "choiring strings" of the Bridge's cable strands and at the same time that this vibrancy/vibration has the power of absolution, originally lodged in the confessional. The "anonymity" bestowed by the Bridge in l. 27 may also belong to the confessional; "raise" in the same line may pun on "raze."

14. Harold Bloom finds a suggestion of a pietà in this line and cites a study by John Irwin speculating that the spatial relationships of "To Brooklyn Bridge" may have been adapted from a painting well known to Crane, El Greco's *The Agony in the Garden*. But the lifting of night in the arms of the Bridge is also the climax of the diurnal motion traced by the poem from daybreak to nightfall. The image is both cosmological and erotic. In its cosmological aspect it completes the condensing of eternity by the starry-sighing beads of (traffic) lights; the lights strung on either side of the Bridge's support towers (its "arms") lift the night to the visionary level of the span as the observer's gaze travels up out of the darkness. This ascent or ascension is also a figurative embrace, whose erotic force recalls the previous stanza's invocation of the lover's cry (which will recur in "The Harbor Dawn").

15. The reference to the shadow of the Bridge may once again identify cruising for lovers with the quest for redemption or mystical love ("Only in darkness is thy shadow clear"). "Shadow" here may carry its older meaning of "image," as in Shelley's "Hymn to Intellectual Beauty": "Sudden, thy shadow fell on me;/I shrieked, and clasped my hands in ecstasy!" (ll. 79–80). Shelley identifies the descent of the shadow with the discovery of his vocation as a poet.

The City's fiery parcels all undone,
Already snow submerges an iron year . . .

O Sleepless as the river under thee,
Vaulting the sea, the prairies' dreaming sod,[16]
Unto us lowliest sometime sweep, descend
And of the curveship lend a myth to God.[17]

16. The sleeplessness of the Bridge continues the religious imagery; the Bridge keeps vigil over the city and the river. The phrase "vaulting the sea" continues the fusion of religious imagery with the architecture of bridges; the Bridge "vaults" the sea in the double sense of encompassing it symbolically and crowning it like a cathedral vault.

17. The concluding apostrophe bidding the Bridge to "sweep" and "descend" reverses the upward sweep of the gull and the sun and at the same time completes the evolution of religious imagery in "To Brooklyn Bridge" by asking the Bridge to reenact the descent of the Holy Spirit on the day of Pentecost as recorded in Acts 2: 2–5: "And suddenly there came a sound from heaven as of a rushing mighty wind, and it filled all the house where they were sitting. And there appeared unto them cloven tongues like as of fire, and it sat upon each of them. And they were all filled with the Holy Ghost, and began to speak with other tongues, as the Spirit gave them utterance." The Bridge, its downward curve combining with the upward curve of the gull to form a perfect circle, becomes the tongue of fire that fulfils the "prophet's pledge" in the mouth of the apostle. Crane coins the word *curveship* to denote this mirror relationship of ascent and descent; the word has homonymic resonance with both "cursive," suggesting the inscription of the poetic Word, and "worship." The curveship "lends a myth" to God as one lends a hand or lends an ear: it restores to the divine the mythic language that modernity has stripped from it. It becomes the modern medium of "accommodation" or (in an older sense of the word) "condescension," by which the divine nature makes itself conformable to the understanding of "us lowliest." In this connection, it is important to note the literalness of Crane's language. The Bridge is invoked, not as a mythical symbol, but as the myth itself in material form.

I. AVE MARIA

Venient annis, saecula seris,
Quibus Oceanus vincula rerum
Laxet et ingens pateat tellus
Tethysque novos detegat orbes
Nec sit terris ultima Thule.

—Seneca

AVE MARIA: The title is related only obliquely to this first section of *The Bridge*, an impressionistic monologue by Columbus recounting his voyage home from the New World in 1493. Crane consulted Columbus's journal for details of the voyage, William H. Prescott's then-standard *History of the Reign of Ferdinand and Isabella* (1885) for the political background, and Waldo Frank's recent *Virgin Spain* (1926) for its conception of Columbus as a poetic visionary intent upon finding a genuinely new world. Originally entitled "Columbus," the text alludes neither to the Catholic prayer *Ave Maria* nor to the musical settings of it by Schubert and Gounod, which Crane might have known. However, as any schoolchild in the 1920s would have been taught, Columbus's three ships were the *Nina*, the *Pinta*, and the *Santa Maria*. The phrase *Ave Maria* may recall, if only as an undertone, another prayer to Mary, *Ave maris stella*—"Hail, Star of the Sea." The Medieval Latin hymn that begins with these words invokes the Virgin as the "gate of heaven," which for Crane's Columbus might suggest an analogue to the New World: "Ave, maris stella, / Dei mater alma, / atque semper virgo, / félix caeli porta" (Hail, star of the sea, / Nurturing Mother of God, / And ever Virgin, / Happy gate of Heaven). A subsequent verse asks Mary as guiding star to "iter para tutum" ("prepare a safe way").

EPIGRAPH: The conclusion to Act 2 of Seneca's *Medea*:

Years will come in the line of ages
In which Ocean will release the chains of things
And the great planet shall stand revealed;
And Tethys will disclose new worlds
Nor shall Thule be the ultimate bound of earth.

The Greek Tethys (Roman Thetis) was one of the twelve Titans, the sister and wife of Oceanus, and the mother of the nymphs of both rivers and oceans. *Thule* is an antique term for Iceland, once thought to be the westernmost boundary of the world. The phrase *ultima Thule*, coined by Virgil in the proem to his *Georgics* in connection with the western expansion of the Roman Empire, proverbially refers to the remotest limit of travel, usually designating a place that can be approached but never reached.

B e with me, Luis de San Angel, now—[1]
Witness before the tides can wrest away[2]
The word I bring, O you who reined my suit
Into the Queen's great heart that doubtful day;[3]
For I have seen now what no perjured breath
Of clown nor sage can riddle or gainsay;—
To you, too, Juan Perez,[4] whose counsel fear
And greed adjourned,—I bring you back Cathay![5]

Here waves climb into dusk on gleaming mail;   9
Invisible waves of the sea,—locks, tendons
Crested and creeping, troughing corridors
That fall back yawning to another plunge.
Slowly the sun's red caravel drops light[6]
Once more behind us. . . . It is morning there—

Columbus,
alone, gazing
toward Spain,
invokes the
presence of
two faithful
partisans of
his quest. . . .

1. Luis de Santángel, the treasurer of the Spanish royal court, used his influence to secure financial backing for Columbus's expedition. See note 3.

2. "Ave Maria" opens *in medias res* on February 13 or 14, 1493, when, according to Columbus's journal, a "great storm" overtook his ship somewhere in the vicinity of the Azores: "The waves were terrible, rising against each other, and so shaking and straining the vessel that she was in danger of being stove in." The whelming tides threatened to "wrest away" the word of Columbus's discoveries. (Crane called attention to the "water-swell rhythm" of the verse in a letter to Waldo Frank, July 26, 1926). After narrowly avoiding being swamped, Columbus ordered that several pilgrimages of thanks be vowed to Marian shrines. Lots were drawn to select the pilgrims: the first one fell to Columbus himself, who, as admiral, drew first (and may have staged the outcome). The whole crew then "made a vow that, on arriving at first land, they would all go in procession, in their shirts, to say their prayers in a church dedicated to Our Lady."

3. The Queen is Isabella I of Spain, who, with her husband King Ferdinand, sponsored Columbus's voyage. The doubtful day occurred in the winter of 1492, when Columbus left the court, his request for funds having been denied after years of postponement. As he rode away, the court treasurer Santángel successfully entreated Isabella to reconsider. Columbus was called back to court that same day.

4. Perez was Columbus's attorney. He helped both in devising arguments in favor of the proposed voyage and in negotiating the final terms of the contract with Ferdinand and Isabella. Perez stood by Columbus's side at a religious ceremony just before Columbus embarked on his first voyage.

5. *Cathay* was the name for China in medieval Europe, famously described as a place of fabulous wealth and power in the widely read *Travels* (1298) of Marco Polo. Columbus carried a copy of the *Travels* with him on his voyage. Intending to reach the unknown eastern boundary of Cathay by his voyage west, he supposed he had done so after making landfall in the Americas—a confusion referred to repeatedly in Crane's text. "The theme of Cathay (its riches, etc.)," Crane wrote, "is ultimately transmuted into a symbol of consciousness, knowledge, spiritual unity" (to Otto Kahn, March 18, 1926).

6. A caravel was a small Spanish sailing vessel; Columbus's ships were caravels. By turning the setting sun (behind the ships as they sail eastward) into a caravel, Crane's metaphor allows the ships to span, like a bridge, the eastern- and westernmost limits of Columbus's voyage.

O where our Indian emperies lie revealed,[7]
Yet lost, all, let this keel one instant yield![8]

I thought of Genoa;[9] and this truth, now proved,[10]   17
That made me exile in her streets, stood me
More absolute than ever—biding the moon
Till dawn should clear that dim frontier,[11] first seen
—The Chan's great continent.[12] . . . Then faith, not fear
Nigh surged me witless. . . . Hearing the surf near—[13]
I, wonder-breathing,[14] kept the watch,—saw
The first palm chevron the first lighted hill.[15]

7. "Our Indian emperies" claims colonial authority for Spain over the New World (where it is symbolically as well as literally morning) in the mistaken guise of India and China. An early draft of this passage, which Crane sent to Waldo Frank (March 20, 1926), reads: "It is morning there,—/O where our other cities, mountains steep/White spires in heaven, yet balanced in this keel!" The other cities, not yet built, and the mountains, not yet witnessed, suggest a vision of the modern continent-spanning America, which Columbus, in Crane's day, was routinely said to have "discovered."

8. The keel refers to the ship as a whole. "Let this keel one instant yield" means "if this keel were to yield for one instant"; yielding to the roiling waves would cause a shipwreck in which Columbus's discovery would be lost along with its discoverer.

9. Columbus was a native of Genoa.

10. "This truth, now proved" refers to the controversial guiding idea behind Columbus' voyage, that a large land mass lay in the west in another hemisphere beyond the Atlantic Ocean. Columbus's mistaken belief that the land he encountered by sailing west was a hitherto unknown part of Asia (hence a "new world") still echoes in the terms "West Indies" and (American) "Indians."

11. Columbus recalls the moment when he first saw the shores of the New World (October 11 and 12, 1492). According to his journal, he became certain that land was near at ten in the evening but had to wait for morning light—to bide the moon—to confirm his surmise. He and his men came ashore on an island of the present-day Bahamas, probably San Salvador, as dawn cleared the dim frontier.

12. "The Chan's great continent": the Far East. *Chan* is an antique form of *Khan*. Columbus believed he had reached the realm of "the Great Khan," that is, the legendary Mongol emperor Kublai Khan, described in Marco Polo's *Travels* and repeatedly mentioned in Columbus's journal. Kublai Khan and the images of exotic wealth and despotic power associated with him embody the conception of the East prevalent in medieval and early modern Europe.

13. Columbus could hear the surf only if he were near land. The sound "nigh surged me witless" with excitement at the prospect that his faith in the truth behind his voyage was about to be vindicated.

14. "Wonder-breathing" recalls the apostrophe to the Bridge in "To Brooklyn Bridge": "Thy cables breathe the North Atlantic still."

15. The image of the palm sighted at dawn is Crane's invention, although Columbus's journal notes "trees very green, and water, and fruits of diverse kinds" as forming his first impression of the island. During the night he and his crew had also seen a flickering light "like a wax candle rising and falling," which Columbus took as a sign of land. The image of the chevron may have been suggested by the letter *Y* (for *Ysabel*) on a banner that Columbus carried with him to shore.

And lowered. And they came out to us crying,   25
"The Great White Birds!"[16] (O Madre María, still
One ship of these thou grantest safe returning;[17]
Assure us through thy mantle's ageless blue!) [18]
And record of more, floating in a casque, [19]
Was tumbled from us under bare poles scudding;[20]
And later hurricanes may claim more pawn. . . .
For here between two worlds, another, harsh,

This third, of water, tests the word; lo, here   33
Bewilderment and mutiny heap whelming
Laughter,[21] and shadow cuts sleep from the heart[22]
Almost as though the Moor's flung scimitar

16. The inhabitants of the island supposedly saw the sails of Columbus's ships as great white birds. Columbus's journal does not record any such incident, but it seems to have been part of Columbian lore. A children's book published in 1892, *The Young Folks' Library of American History: The Story of Columbus*, by Mara L. Pratt, recounts the anecdote thus: "In the morning . . . a throng of natives plunged into the water and swam to the ships' sides. Kindly they were received, and after a short visit, during which they sharply inspected the "strange white birds" as they called the ships, they swam back, delighted as children with the bits of colored beads that Columbus had given them." The story, repeated in numerous school textbooks with the obvious intent of demonstrating European superiority, may have been spun from an incident that Columbus does report: some of the local people, swimming to his ship some days later, asked (or so he interpreted the question) if he had come from heaven. Crane's inclusion of the great white birds seems meant to link Columbus's ships with the gull whose flight opens "To Brooklyn Bridge."

17. This plea to the Virgin Mother returns to the present after Columbus's flashback to the outbound voyage. With two of his original three ships remaining, Columbus prays that at least one may complete the voyage home.

18. Blue is Mary's color in traditional iconography; she is often depicted wearing a blue mantle. In the middle ages, the blue paint involved was made with lapis lazuli, a stone so precious it rivaled gold in value; its use was considered an act of glorification.

19. Anticipating possible shipwreck in the storm, Columbus wrote "as good an account as he could of all he had discovered," sealed the document tightly in waxed cloth, and ordered it to be thrown into the sea in a large wooden barrel, Crane's "casque." Anyone finding the barrel was entreated to deliver its contents to Isabella and Ferdinand.

20. Bare poles: the sails of a ship are lowered during a storm.

21. Columbus's outbound journey was troubled by unrest among his crew. In his journal he complains of the "trouble caused by the sailors and people of his company, who all with one voice declared their intention to return and protested they would rise against him." In November 1492, Martin Alonso Pinzon, the captain of the *Pinta*, withdrew his ship from the expedition "in disobedience to and against the wish of the Admiral, and out of avarice." Pinzon returned in early January 1493 but failed to placate Columbus, who "could not understand the insolence and disloyalty with which Pinzon had treated him."

22. Columbus's journal records that, between Wednesday, February 12, 1493, and Saturday, February 16, "he had not slept nor been able to sleep . . . and his legs were very sore from long exposure to the wet and cold." The message in a barrel had been dispatched on February 14.

Found more than flesh to fathom in its fall.[23]
Yet under tempest-lash and surfeitings
Some inmost sob, half-heard, dissuades the abyss,[24]
Merges the wind in measure to the waves,

Series on series, infinite,—till eyes   41
Starved wide on blackened tides, accrete—enclose
This turning rondure whole, [25] this crescent ring
Sun-cusped and zoned with modulated fire[26]
Like pearls that whisper through the Doge's hands[27]
—Yet no delirium of jewels! O Fernando,

23. Columbus once more worries that his death at sea would mean the obliteration of his discoveries. This symbolic death would be worse than its physical counterpart; it would represent the cutting off of "more than flesh," namely, the geographical and cosmological truth he had set out to prove. The blow would come as if at the hands of the Moors, whose power in Spain ended under the reign of Isabella and Ferdinand; the Moor's iconic flung scimitar, linked to the whelming sea by Crane's use of "fathom" to mean "dig into," would exact revenge even as it fell in defeat.

24. "Some inmost sob" may refer to the personal vows made by Columbus's crew during the storm in case the communal vows of pilgrimage went unfulfilled: "for no one expected to escape, holding themselves for lost, owing to the fearful weather." The power of a sob made "under tempest-lash" to "dissuade the abyss" imparts a penitential cast to weathering the storm, as if the ships were enduring flagellation.

25. The "turning rondure" is the earth in its aspect as globe and celestial sphere; Crane's choice of words echoes Whitman's famous lines from section 5 of "Passage to India": "O vast Rondure, swimming in space, / Cover'd all over with visible power and beauty . . . / With inscrutable purpose, some hidden prophetic intention, / Now first it seems my thought begins to span thee." In section 3 Whitman identifies the completion of the Transcontinental Railroad in 1869, which linked the east and west coasts of the United States, as the "verification" of Columbus's dream, to which his poem's title is a reference.

26. The "crescent ring / Sun-cusp'd" is the earth at sunset, specifically, the curve of the horizon at sea bisected by the setting sun. In architecture, a cusp is the point formed by the intersection of two arcs; Crane's image divides the crescent of the horizon / ring into equal portions joined by the sun, as cusp, at the center. The allusion is probably to the arches of gothic churches, extending the text's network of religious associations. "Zoned" here is used in its antique sense of "girdled, wrapped around with"; "modulated fire," literally the red of the sunset, alludes to the highest of the heavenly spheres in traditional cosmology, the empyrean, the realm of pure light and fire.

27. *Doge* was the title of the chief magistrate of the Republics of Venice and Genoa from 697 to 1797. Crane's reference is to the Doge of Venice, who, in a ceremony dating to the twelfth century, symbolically married the sea each year by throwing a wedding ring blessed by the Pope into the Adriatic. Crane's image expands the wedding ring to the crescent ring of earth, but with a note of admonition, perhaps a consequence of the penitential ordeal, sounded in the following lines.

Take of that eastern shore, this western sea,
Yet yield thy God's, thy Virgin's charity![28]

—Rush down the plentitude, and you shall see   49
Isaiah counting famine on this lee![29]

* * *

An herb, a stray branch among salty teeth,
The jellied weeds that drag the shore,[30]—perhaps
Tomorrow's moon will grant us Saltes Bar—[31]
Palos again,—a land cleared of long war.[32]

28. Addressing King Ferdinand, Crane's Columbus issues a warning, obviously in vain, against the greedy exploitation of Spain's colonial "possessions"; his admonition echoes Whitman's dismissal, in section 6 of "Passage to India," of a "mere Doge of Venice now wedding the Adriatic" in favor of a world-spanning "marriage of continents, climates, and oceans. . . . Europe to Asia, Africa join'd, and they to the New World, / The lands, geographies, dancing before you, holding a festival garland, / As brides and bridegrooms hand in hand." The dance and the marriage are traditional representations of cosmic harmony; Crane returns to them throughout *The Bridge*.

29. The admonition to Ferdinand concludes with the figure of Isaiah, taken to embody the poet-prophet who denounces arrogance, greed, and spiritual emptiness. Crane may not have had a specific passage in mind, but Isaiah 58: 6–7 is a likely candidate: "Is not this the fast that I have chosen? To loose the bands of wickedness, to undo the heavy burdens, and to let the oppressed go free, and that ye break every yoke? Is it not to deal thy bread to the hungry, and that thou bring the poor that are cast out to thy house? When thou seest the naked, that thou cover him; and that thou hide not thyself from thy own flesh?"

30. The "jellied weeds that drag that shore" suggest the Sargasso Sea, a "sea within a sea" in the North Atlantic surrounded by ocean currents and strewn with free-floating seaweed. Columbus crossed the Sargasso Sea in the vicinity of Bermuda during his outbound voyage and recorded in his journal that: "the sea being smooth and calm, the crew began to murmur, saying . . . that the wind would never blow so that they could return to Spain. Afterwards the sea rose very much, without wind, which astonished them." Columbus added that the high sea was "very necessary to me, such as had not appeared but in the time of the Jews when they went out of Egypt and murmured against Moses, who delivered them from captivity."

31. Saltes is an island formed by two arms of the river Odiel near the town of Huelva in Andalusia, in extreme southwestern Spain. Columbus departed Spain via Saltes bar from the port of Palos de la Frontera in Huelva on August 3, 1492, and recrossed the bar en route to Palos on his return journey in 1493—the last event described in his journal.

32. On January 2, 1492, Ferdinand and Isabella "cleared the land of long war" by conquering Granada, the last Spanish stronghold of the Moors. The surrender of Granada completed the *reconquista*—the "reconquest" of Muslim Spain by the Catholic Monarchs—and also initiated the expulsion of the Jews, who had enjoyed religious tolerance under the Moors. Columbus witnessed the Moorish King Boabdil emerge from the city gates to kiss the hands of Ferdinand and Isabella as the couple formally took possession of the Alhambra as a Spanish court.

Some Angelus[33] environs the cordage tree;[34]
Dark waters onward shake the dark prow free.

*   *   *

O Thou who sleepest on Thyself, apart   57
Like ocean athwart lanes of death and birth,[35]
And all the eddying breath between dost search
Cruelly with love thy parable of man,—[36]
Inquisitor![37] incognizable Word
Of Eden and the enchained Sepulchre[38]

33. The *Angelus* is a Catholic prayer commemorating the Annunciation, the angel Gabriel's appearance to Mary with the word that she would conceive a divine child. The opening verse, "Angelus Domini nuntiavit Mariae. / Et concepit de Spiritu Sancto" ("The angel of the Lord announced unto Mary. / And she conceived by the Holy Spirit"), places the angel in the role of poet-prophet, occupied in turn by Columbus, Whitman, and the Crane who speaks as author of *The Bridge*. The angel's utterance, following the quoted couplet, is the *Ave Maria*: "Ave Maria, gratia plena, Dominus tecum" ("Hail Mary, full of grace, the Lord is with thee").

34. "Cordage tree" refers figuratively to Columbus's ship via its masts and rigging and, proleptically, to Brooklyn Bridge via its suspension cables. Environed by the *Angelus*, the tree may also—the usage is traditional—suggest the cross.

35. From this point on, "Ave Maria" becomes a reworking of Whitman's "Prayer of Columbus" (1874), a companion piece to "Passage to India." Whitman's Columbus, in penitential old age, declares his lifelong dedication to God and, though in an agony of self-doubt, assumes the mantle of the poet-prophet who envisions "newer, better worlds": "Shadowy vast shapes smile through the earth and sky, / And on the distant waves sail countless ships, / And anthems in new tongues I hear saluting me." The God of Whitman's poem is unknowably remote (in Crane's terms, he both "sleeps on himself apart" and incarnates an "incognizable Word"), and yet he becomes fully present in the form or figure of the sea. Hence the cry of Whitman's Columbus to "put forth myself . . . once more to Thee, / Breathe, bathe myself once more in Thee, commune in thee," which Crane echoes, but reverses, when he likens God's apartness to that of the ocean "athwart"—straddling—the cycles of death and birth and the eddying of breath in between.

36. "Thy parable of man" does not refer to a parable *about* man but to mankind itself *as* a parable. In Genesis 1:26–27, man is made in the image of God and is, as such, both a true and a false representation of the divine nature. Like the parables of Jesus, man as parable is necessarily obscure, even, Crane suggests, to his Creator.

37. Ferdinand and Isabella established the Spanish Inquisition to root out, expel, or execute heretics, primarily Jewish and Muslim converts to Catholicism who were thought to practice their original faiths in secret. Crane's Columbus identifies God as an Inquisitor presumably because of the cruel ordeals by which he "searches"—tests the faith—of his parable of man.

38. In theological terms, God as the Word (Greek *logos*, also reason) is both the ultimate mystery and the ultimate truth: "In the beginning was the Word. And the Word was with God, and the Word was God" (John 1:1.) In historical terms, the Word is incognizable because the New World is still only a distant promise; the lost Eden has not yet been regained and the Holy Sepulchre, Christ's empty tomb in Jerusalem, is still "enchained," that is, in the hands of the Moors. Whitman's Columbus acknowledges a similar uncertainty: "Is it the prophet's thought I speak, or am I raving? / What do I know of life? what of myself?" In "Atlantis," the last poem in *The Bridge* (although the first to be written), the incognizable Word is transmuted into Brooklyn Bridge as "steeled Cognizance."

Into thy steep savannahs, burning blue,[39]
Utter to loneliness the sail is true.

Who grindest oar, and arguing the mast   65
Subscribest holocaust of ships, O Thou
Within whose primal scan consummately
The glistening seignories of Ganges swim;—[40]
Who sendest greeting by the corposant,[41]
And Teneriffe's garnet—flamed it in a cloud,[42]
Urging through night our passage to the Chan;—
Te Deum laudamus, for thy teeming span![43]

Of all the amplitude that time explores,   73
A needle in the sight, suspended north,—
Yielding by inference and discard, faith

39. "Burning blue" describes the sea beneath Columbus's ship (already associated with the Virgin's mantle) and anticipates the last line of *The Bridge*: "Whispers antiphonal in azure swing." "Thy steep savannahs" are the tropical grasslands of the New World, to which Columbus's sail remains true through every ordeal. Following this declaration, the poem becomes a hymn of Thanksgiving.

40. Grinding the oar and arguing the mast suggest the penitential "tempest-lash" with which the poem begins; the "holocaust of ships" is the history of shipwreck, from which Columbus's expedition also suffered. (Like the phrase "burning blue," the term *holocaust*, denoting a great fire, has connotations that are taken up at the end of "Ave Maria.") The "primal span" is the link between the worlds of east and west, Europe and Asia, the latter encompassing the holy river Ganges, which Columbus believed he had discovered.

41. Also known as "St. Elmo's fire," the corposant is a flamelike blue or violet glow often seen atop the masts of sailing ships during a thunderstorm. Corposants were richly laden with maritime lore and superstition and were sometimes regarded as the souls of dead sailors; the term *corposant* derives from the Latin *corpus sanctum*, "holy body," which for Crane's Columbus would make them divine visitations linked to the Incarnation. Seen aloft, corposants (especially in pairs) portended good luck. The question of their prophetic value dominates the treatment of corposants in "The Candle," Melville's chapter on them in *Moby-Dick*.

42. Tenerife is the largest of the Canary Islands, near the coast of Africa. Columbus witnessed a volcanic eruption there—his journal records a "great fire issu[ing] from the mountain"—on his outbound voyage. Crane's phrase "flamed in a cloud" is a condensed allusion to another divine visitation: the appearance of God as a pillar of cloud by day and pillar of fire by night to lead the Israelites during their exodus from Egypt (*Exodus* 13:21).

43. *Te Deum Laudamus* ("God We Praise Thee") is a hymn traditionally sung on occasions of public rejoicing. When Columbus returned from his voyage of discovery, the entire city of Palos accompanied him and his men to church, where they sang the *Te Deum* in celebration.

And true appointment from the hidden shoal:[44]
This disposition that thy night relates
From Moon to Saturn in one sapphire wheel: [45]
The orbic wake of thy once whirling feet,
Elohim, still I hear thy sounding heel! [46]

White toil of heaven's cordons,[47] mustering   81
In holy rings all sails charged to the far
Hushed gleaming fields and pendant seething wheat

44. From "a needle in the sight" to the end of the poem, the syntax is tangled even by Crane's loose standards. As his ships neared the New World, Columbus encountered the phenomenon known as variation of the compass: the difference—variable by location—between true north, oriented to the earth's geographical pole, and magnetic north, oriented to the earth's magnetic pole. Confronted with the disparity, Columbus probably used dead reckoning to set his course, thus allowing inference and discard—that is, logical elimination—to justify his faith in his heading and protect his ships from hidden shoals (whether literal or metaphorical).

45. The image of the sapphire wheel once again invokes the traditional cosmology, derived from Ptolemy, of the heavens as a system of concentric spheres. The first seven of the ten spheres encompassed the "seven planets" from the moon to Saturn; the sapphire wheel is the tenth sphere, the empyrean, which bounds the whole.

46. *Elohim* is a Hebrew epithet for the Old Testament God. God's wake is "orbic" both in conformity to the spherical form of the traditional heavens and in reference to the heavenly wheels seen in a vision by the Old Testament prophet Ezekiel. Ezekiel's wheels, composed of living creatures who appear out of a whirlwind, also incorporate the image of divine prophetic fire, which becomes increasingly prominent as "Ave Maria" unfolds: "Their appearance was like burning coals of fire, and like the appearance of lamps; it went up and down among the living ceatures, and the fire was bright. . . . And when the living creatures went, the wheels went by them. . . . And when they went, I heard the noise of their wings, like the noise of great waters, as the voice of the Almighty, the voice of speech" (Ezekiel 1: 13, 19, 24). The reference to Ezekiel's wheels may extend to the reworking of them in Shelley's *Prometheus Unbound* (1819), where they assumes a similar apocalyptic value: "[Now] rushes, with loud and whirlwind harmony, / A sphere, which is as many thousand spheres, / Solid as crystal, yet through all its mass / Flow, as through empty space, music and light" (4.236–40). Another gloss on God's whirling feet and sounding heel is the conception of cosmic motion as a circular dance, another element of Greek cosmology widely adopted by Christian Europe. According to the second-century dialogue "On the Dance," by Lucian, "Dance came into being contemporaneously with the primal origin of the universe, making her appearance together with Love—the love that is age-old. In fact, the concord of the heavenly spheres, the interlacing of the errant planets with the fixed stars, their rhythmic agreement and timed harmony, are proofs that Dance was primordial."

47. Heavens' cordons are probably the boundary lines of the celestial spheres metaphorically understood as ropes or lines; the cordons gather (muster) the sails of ships devoted to knowledge along the earth's meridians—the great circles passing longitudinally from pole to pole—to form a "holy circle" in which the spheres of terrestrial geography mirror those of the traditional cosmos and echo the ring of cosmic marriage alluded to earlier in the poem. The phrase "hushed gleaming fields and pendent seething wheat / Of knowledge" is glossed in n. 48; the geographical gloss resumes in n. 50. The difficulty of Crane's language here, not to say its confusion, makes any gloss somewhat conjectural.

Of knowledge,[48]—round thy brows unhooded now
—The kindled Crown! Acceded of the poles
And biassed by full sails, meridians reel
Thy purpose[49]—still one shore beyond desire!
The sea's green crying towers a-sway, Beyond

And kingdoms
          naked in the
              trembling heart—
     Te Deum laudamus
             O Thou Hand of Fire[50]

48. The image of gleaming fields and seething wheat is prophetic; the knowledge gained by Columbus makes possible the fertility and abundance of latter-day America. Crane's phrasing suggests a loose paraphrase of the "amber waves of grain" and "fruited plain," both objects of God's grace, in "America, the Beautiful."

49. The earth's newly mapped meridians (now circling the globe according to Columbus's erroneous reckoning) are crossed on the diagonal ("biased") by the full sails passing between the Old World and the New. The great wheeling (reeling) system of circles resembles the wheels within wheels of Ezekiel and Shelley, which constitute God's kindled crown; the meridian lines crisscrossed by the sails resemble the harp-like cables of the Bridge.

50. "O Thou Hand of Fire" alludes to section 3, "The Fire Sermon, of Eliot's *The Waste Land*, where the speaker finds himself burning in St. Augustine's cauldron of unholy loves:

To Carthage then I came

Burning burning burning burning
O Lord Thou pluckest me out
O Lord Thou pluckest burning

burning

In Crane the burning itself becomes redemptive; the hand of God does not redeem the speaker from the fires of lust but writes with the fires of prophecy, whose material trace is the text of the poem. As Ezekiel's "voice of speech" becomes inspired writing, as the mantle of the ancient prophet passes to the modern poet, the Pentecostal tongues of flame and, perhaps, the burning coal placed in the mouth of Isaiah by the angel of God (Isaiah 6:6–8) become the "Hand of Fire."

II. POWHATAN'S DAUGHTER

"Pocahuntus, a well-featured but wanton young girl . . . of the age of eleven or twelve years, get the boyes forth with her into the market place, and make them wheele, falling on their hands, turning their heels upwards, whom she would followe, and wheele so herself, naked as she was, all the fort over."

POWHATAN'S DAUGHTER: In a letter to Otto Kahn, Crane says that Powhatan's daughter, the legendary Pocahontas, is "the mythological nature-symbol chosen to represent the physical body of the continent, or the soil" (September 12, 1927). He adds that Pocahontas in this role resembles the Teutonic earth goddess Hertha. This use of the Native American as a means of "finding," or rather creating, America is mirrored by other early-twentieth-century writers, including Crane's friend the journalist and social philosopher Waldo Frank. In his *The Rediscovery of America*, Frank asserts that "Our root is in the red men, and our denial of this is a disease within us." Crane's conception of Pocahontas is close to that of Vachel Lindsay in the latter's 1917 poem "Our Mother Pocahontas":

> John Rolfe is not our ancestor.
> We rise from out the soul of her
> Held in native wonderland,
> While the sun's rays kissed her hand,
> In the springtime,
> In Virginia,
> Our Mother, Pocahontas. (ll. 1–7)

Powhatan was the ruler of the Algonquin Indian tribe in Tidewater, Virginia. His chiefdom covered nearly all of eastern Virginia when Jamestown was founded in 1607. Pocahontas (1595–1617) was regarded as a peacemaker between the Native Americans and the English. Much of the narrative around her has been too embellished and mythologized to sort out fact from fiction with confidence.

EPIGRAPH: Quoted from *A Historie of Travaile into Virginia*, by William Strachey, an English colonial historian and secretary for the Virginia Company who spent time in the colonies starting in 1610. According to R. W. B. Lewis, Crane took the quotation from Kay Boyle's review of William Carlos Williams's *The American Grain*, which quotes Strachey at length. It is doubtful whether Strachey ever saw Pocahontas. His description of her clearly mirrors the account of Captain John Smith, from whom Strachey may simply have lifted his portrait. Crane essentially borrowed a mythic record for his own mythic use.

THE HARBOR DAWN

Insistently through sleep—a tide of voices—
They meet you listening midway in your dream,
The long, tired sounds, fog-insulated noises:[1]
Gongs in white surplices, beshrouded wails,[2]
Far strum of fog horns . . . signals dispersed in veils.

And then a truck will lumber past the wharves
As winch engines begin throbbing on some deck;
Or a drunken stevedore's howl and thud below
Comes echoing alley-upward through dim snow.

And if they take your sleep away sometimes   10
They give it back again.[3] Soft sleeves of sound

400 years and
more . . . or is
it from the
soundless shore
of sleep that
time

THE HARBOR DAWN: The title may allude to Waldo Frank's proclamation of an "American Dawn," an emerging modern aesthetic connected with a new awareness of the American land.

　1. The image of fog frames the poem; it may echo any number of similar images in Eliot, especially that of the "Unreal City / Under the brown fog of a winter noon" in "The Fire Sermon" from *The Waste Land* ("The Harbor Dawn" is also set in winter). An even more likely resonance is with Carl Sandburg's once-famous poem "Fog," published in 1916:

> The fog comes
> on little cat feet.
>
> It sits looking
> over harbor and city
> on silent haunches
> and then moves on.

　2. Surplices are vestments used in Catholic ritual: loose-fitting white ecclesiastical gowns with wide sleeves, draped over a cassock. They are worn by the choir (here the "tide of voices" shrouded by the white fog), by those in processionals, and by lower clergy administering the sacraments. The gong suggests Eastern religious ritual, in keeping with the theme of Cathay introduced in "Ave Maria"; Crane thus invokes, but also reverses (for this is a love poem), Eliot's avowed "collocation of . . . two representatives of eastern and western asceticism" (the Buddha and St. Augustine) in "The Fire Sermon."

　3. Crane wrote to his mother on February 10, 1925: "I haven't had 6 hours of solid sleep for three nights, what with the bedlam of bells, grunts, whistles, screams and groans of all the river and harbor buoys, which have kept up an incessant grinding program as noisome as the midnight passing into new year. Just like the mouth of hell, not being able to see six feet from the window and yet hearing all the weird jargon constantly." An earlier letter (November 16, 1924) supplies the contrary: "All night long there were distant tinklings, buoy bells and siren warnings from river craft. It was like wakening into a dream-land in the early dawn—one wondered where one was with only a milky light in the window and that vague music from a hidden world." The imagery of music heard at a distance found its way into "The Harbor Dawn," where it anticipates the images of cosmic harmony in the (already written) concluding poem, "Atlantis."

Attend the darkling harbor, the pillowed bay;
Somewhere out there in blankness steam

Spills into steam, and wanders, washed away
—Flurried by keen fifings, eddied
Among distant chiming buoys—adrift. The sky,

Cool feathery fold, suspends, distills
This wavering slumber . . . Slowly—
Immemorially the window, the half-covered chair
Ask nothing but this sheath of pallid air.   20

And you beside me,[4] blessed now while sirens   *recalls you to*
Sing to us, stealthily weave us into day—[5]   *your love,*
Serenely now, before day claims our eyes[6]   *there in a*

4. The beloved, as the marginal gloss explains, is an incarnation of Pocahontas, whose body (regardless of who incarnates it, and regardless of whether Crane is personally thinking of a man or a woman here) is coextensive with the American continent, shortly to be traversed in "The River" and "The Dance."

5. The sirens occupy at least three levels of meaning. At the most literal, they represent the drifting sounds of foghorns and other "fog-insulated noises" that accompany the poet in and out of sleep. Figuratively, these sounds suggest the sirens of Homer's *Odyssey*: creatures with the heads of women and the bodies of birds who lured sailors to shipwreck and death with their enchanting songs—always heard at a distance. Odysseus has himself bound to the mast of his ship in order to hear the sirens' song without yielding to their lure. Crane invokes the Homeric sirens with a characteristic reversal; the sirens of "The Harbor Dawn" are the benign messengers of a "hidden world" (see n. 3) that "weave us into day," completing or continuing rather than nullifying an Odyssean voyage. In this respect, they merge with the heavenly sirens described in the tenth book of Plato's *Republic*, who with their song control the movement of the celestial spheres. (Crane explicitly alludes to Plato in the epigraph to "Atlantis.") Plato's Pythagorean myth represents the spheres as wheels turned on a spindle; a siren occupied each wheel, singing a tone that harmonized with the tones of her sisters, while the three Fates simultaneously wove the destinies of men. When Crane's sirens "weave us into day," their action harmonizes with the weaving of the fates, which on this occasion has a "blessed" outcome—again a reversal of the classical norm. The music of the spheres was thought to be inaudible to human ears, but poetic tradition held that its sound could be heard momentarily in states of special blessedness.

6. The phrase "Before day claims our eyes"—presumably turning them back from the world of dream, vision, and prophecy to the mundanity of ordinary life—identifies "The Harbor Dawn" as an aubade, a poem of lovers' parting at morning. In section 3 of *Song of Myself*, Whitman describes a similar dawn scene, which, like Crane's, replaces the aubade's traditional tone of regret with a celebratory rapture: "I am satisfied—I see, dance, laugh, sing: / As the hugging and loving bedfellow sleeps at my side through the night and withdraws at the peep of the day with stealthy tread."

Your cool arms murmurously about me lay.[7]

While myriad snowy hands are clustering at the panes—[8]

your hands within my hands are deeds;
my tongue upon your throat—singing[9]

arms close; eyes wide, undoubtful
> *dark*
>> *drink the dawn—*
a forest shudders in your hair![10]   30

—*with whom?*

The window goes blond slowly. Frostily clears.

7. The murmurousness of the beloved's arms, echoed by the "singing arms" of the italicized section to follow, translate the song of the heavenly sirens into explicitly erotic terms, which fold over to identify the mystic or cosmic marriage with poetic inspiration.

8. The "myriad snowy hands" at the window anticipate the maternal memory recorded in the next poem, "Van Winkle": the mother's smile, another legacy of Pocahontas, "flickered through the snow screen, blindly / It forsook her at the doorway, it was gone / Before I had left the window. It / Did not return with the kiss in the hall."

9. The use of italics to isolate a moment of ecstatic union probably derives from Whitman's "Out of the Cradle Endlessly Rocking," which likewise uses italics (though more extensively) to house an image of mystic marriage and poetic inspiration through the union (and separation) of two songbirds on the Long Island shore. Crane's subsequent image of "cold gulls" aloft with the sun, recalling the sweeping gull of "To Brooklyn Bridge," continues the chain of associations.

10. The forest in the beloved's hair recalls Baudelaire's "The Head of Hair" ("Le Chevelure"), whose speaker apostrophizes the hair of his beloved as an "aromatic forest." To a significant degree, "The Harbor Dawn" forms an extended paraphrase of Baudelaire's third stanza, which identifies the flowing hair with

> A resonant harbor where my soul can drink
> The perfume, sound, and color of great waves;
> Where vessels, gliding in the moiré and gold,
> Open their wide arms to embrace the shine
> Of a pure sky where trembles eternal warmth.
> (My translation)

The image of the forest also alludes to the earth goddess Hertha, with whom Crane identified Pocahontas partly on the basis of reading Swinburne's poem "Hertha." Swinburne's goddess describes herself as the "life-tree," the source of all things:

> These too have their part in me,
> As I too in these;
> Such fire is at heart in me,
> Such sap is this tree's
> Which has in it all sounds and all secrets of infinite lands and of seas.

From Cyclopean towers across Manhattan waters[11]
—Two-three bright window-eyes aglitter, disk
The sun, released—aloft with cold gulls hither.[12]

The fog leans one last moment on the sill.
Under the mistletoe of dreams, a star—[13]

Who is the

woman with

11. The "Cyclopean towers" continue the identification of the poet with the questing Odysseus—who, not coincidentally, was also on a voyage seeking reunion with his spouse, Penelope, the Homeric equivalent of Crane's Pocahontas. The Cyclops was a belligerent one-eyed giant whom Odysseus both fooled and blinded. The image of Cyclopean towers also suggests that modern urban life, symbolized by the skyscrapers of Manhattan, suffers from limited, one-dimensional vision.

12. The purblindness of the towers is reversed when their windows reflect the rising sun as it joins the gulls aloft and mirror the poet's gaze from his own window across the East River ("Manhattan waters"). In addition to their counterparts in Whitman's "Crossing Brooklyn Ferry," the gulls here may recall "the great gull" of William Carlos Williams's "Advent," the first poem in the sequence *The Wanderer*, published in 1914. Like Baudelaire's "The Head of Hair," "Advent" may form a model that "The Harbor Dawn" sought to rework:

> But one day, crossing the ferry
> With the great towers of Manhattan before me,
> Out at the prow with the sea wind blowing,
> I had been wearying many questions
> Which she had put on to try me:
> How shall I be a mirror to this modernity?
> When lo! in a rush, dragging
> A blunt boat on the yielding river—
> Suddenly I saw her! . . .
> . . . And with that a great sea-gull
> Went to the left, vanishing with a wild cry—
> But in my mind all the persons of godhead
> Followed after.

13. The star in "The Harbor Dawn" anticipates that of "The Dance": "And one star, swinging, [took] its place, alone . . . / Until, immortally, it bled into the dawn." The star is literally the Morning Star, the planet Venus, the brightest star in the sky and the traditional bringer of dawn (its Greek name, Phosphorus, means "light-bringer"; the associated deity, son of the goddess of dawn, was a young man whose beauty was said to rival that of Venus/ Aphrodite). Given the reference to "the mistletoe of dreams," however, which brings to mind the Christmas custom of kissing under the mistletoe, the star may also suggest the star of Bethlehem. Another and perhaps stronger resonance, also associated with cycles of death and rebirth, is with the Norse myth of the demigod Baldur, who dreamed of an early death. To secure his safety, his mother appealed to every being and force in nature to spare him, but she forgot the mistletoe. This loophole (the Norse version of Achilles' heel) allowed the trickster god Loki to fool Baldur's blind twin brother into striking him with an arrow made of mistletoe. Baldur's death brought winter into the world, but the gods subsequently intervened to resurrect him.

As though to join us at some distant hill—
Turns in the waking west and goes to sleep.[14]

us in the
dawn? . . .
whose is the
flesh our feet
have moved
upon?

14. The "waking west" again recalls Frank's "American dawn," associated with the history and promise of transcontinental movement (reinforced here by the image in the marginal gloss of the beloved's flesh as the earth on which "our" feet have moved). The (literal) disorientation of dawn from east to west inverts the traditional association of westward movement with death.

2. Manhattan Skyline from the Bridge, 1918.

VAN WINKLE

M acadam, gun-grey as the tunny's belt,[1]
Leaps from Far Rockaway to Golden Gate:[2]

Listen![3] the miles a hurdy-gurdy grinds—[4]

Down gold arpeggios mile on mile unwinds.[5]

Streets spread

past store and

factory—sped

by sunlight

VAN WINKLE: The title character is, of course, Rip Van Winkle, of Washington Irving's famous story of the same name (1819). Van Winkle falls asleep in the Catskill Mountains and wakes up twenty years later; in Crane's version the nap lasts rather longer, leaving Rip a citizen of the modern metropolis. The poem makes several glancing allusions to details from the story, noted below. Crane may or may not have known that Irving took vacations at a celebrated seaside hotel in Far Rockaway and that he planned to write a biography of Columbus.

1. "Tunny": tuna. The image, like the highway, unites land and sea in a single leaping curve, like the arc of the Bridge in "To Brooklyn Bridge." Compare the first section of Whitman's "Starting from Paumanok" (the title refers to the Indian name for Long Island), which begins "Starting from fish-shape Paumanok where I was born" and ends, after a continent-spanning series of images, "Solitary, singing in the West, I strike up for a New World."

2. The macadam highway "bridging" the east and west coasts of the United States gives modern material form to the country's nineteenth-century credo of "manifest destiny"—the supposedly inevitable westward expansion joining the Atlantic to the Pacific. The Golden Gate here is not the famous bridge, which was completed in 1937, five years after Crane's death, but the strait dividing San Francisco Bay from the ocean. It was so named in 1846 by John Charles Fremont in expectation of the inflow of riches from trade with Asia, an origin that links its naming in the poem both to Columbus's dream of Cathay and to the nineteenth-century clipper ship trade recalled in "Cutty Sark." ("Golden Gate" is a play on "Golden Horn," a name for the Bosporus or Hellespont, the Turkish strait alluded to in the epigraph of "Three Songs.") Far Rockaway, at the tip of the Rockaway peninsula on the Long Island shore, not only marks the eastern edge of the country but may also evoke Whitman's depiction of the "slapping waves" and "lone singer" in a poem whose title Crane's choice of place name may echo, "Out of the Cradle Endlessly Rocking." In his *Specimen Days*, Whitman notes that "at Rockaway and far east along the Hamptons, the beach makes right on the island, the sea dashing up without intervention."

3. As Irving's Rip starts to descend from the Catskill peak where he has taken refuge from work (and his nagging wife), he is mysteriously accosted by "a voice from a distance, hallooing, 'Rip Van Winkle! Rip Van Winkle!'"

4. "Hurdy-gurdy": the barrel organ, widely associated with Italian immigrants playing on street corners; it is thus a distant echo of Columbus's voyage. A similar transposition appears in "The Tunnel," in the person of the crudely named "Wop washerwoman."

5. As the marginal gloss indicates, the transcontinental movement of the arpeggios is "sped by sunlight"; their gold, like that of the sun, moves across the country from east to west. The unwinding of the miles links both the highway and the sound of the barrel organ to Whitman's equally continent-spanning open road; the poem of that name at one point also links the leaping of distance to a musical motion: "The earth expanding right hand and left hand, / The picture alive, every part in its best light, / The music falling in where it is wanted, and stopping where it is not wanted, / The cheerful voice of the open road" ("Song of the Open Road," ll. 39–42). Crane, however, counterpoints Whitman's future-oriented journey with a movement of both personal and historical memory.

Times earlier, when you hurried off to school,

—It is the same hour though a later day—[6]

You walked with Pizarro in a copybook,[7]

And Cortes rode up, reining tautly in—[8]

Firmly as coffee grips the taste,—and away!

and her

smile . . .

There was Priscilla's cheek close in the wind,[9]   10

And Captain Smith,[10] all beard and certainty,

And Rip Van Winkle bowing by the way,—

"Is this Sleepy Hollow, friend—?" And he—[11]

Like Memory,

she is time's

And Rip forgot the office hours,   *truant, shall*

and he forgot the pay;[12]   *take you by*

Van Winkle sweeps a tenement   *the hand . . .*

way down on Avenue A,—[13]

6. Whether real or imagined, the sound of the hurdy-gurdy triggers a Proustian involuntary memory of childhood, mediated initially by the lessons (or legends) in American history that any child of Crane's generation would have learned in grade school.

7. Francisco Pizarro (1475–1541): a conquistador who seized the Inca empire for Spain, hence an explorer and adventurer in the mold of the poem's Columbus and commonly represented as a hero in the schoolbooks of Crane's America.

8. Hernán Cortés (1485–1547): a conquistador who won Mexico for Spain—another purported hero of New World settlement. A legend widely taught in Crane's day claimed that the Indians regarded Cortés and his men on horseback as gods.

9. Priscilla Mullen, from Henry Wadsworth Longfellow's poem "The Courtship of Miles Standish" (1858), once a schoolroom classic. The poem mythologizes John Alden (1599?–1687) as the first Pilgrim to set foot on Plymouth Rock and as the stand-in for Miles Standish in the latter's suit for Priscilla Mullen's hand in marriage. The historical Mullen married Alden in 1623.

10. John Smith (baptized 1580, died 1631): an English explorer who was captured by the Algonquin Indians under chief Powhatan in colonial Virginia; according to his own account, Smith was saved from death by Pocahontas, Powhatan's daughter. Pocahontas eventually married Smith and died shortly after emigrating with him to England.

11. The protagonist of Irving's "The Legend of Sleepy Hollow" shares the poet's surname: "In this by-place of nature, there abode, in a remote place of American history, that is to say, some thirty years since, a worthy wight of the name of Ichabod Crane; who sojourned, or, as he expressed it, 'tarried,' in Sleepy Hollow, for the purpose of instructing the children of the vicinity." The Crane of the story is pursued (or so he thinks) by the ghostly Headless Horseman, who, local legend claims, is forbidden to cross a bridge built near a church; the "church bridge" becomes one of the story's central images. Irving links the legend of the Headless Horseman to the Indian heritage of the vicinity, a theme Crane will develop in detail in "The Dance": "Some say that . . . an old Indian chief, the prophet or wizard of his tribe, held his powwows there before the country was discovered by Master Hendrick Hudson."

12. Irving's Rip is an energetic loafer, helpful to others but averse to earning his own keep: "The great error in Rip's composition was an insuperable aversion to all kinds of profitable labor."

13. Avenue A: the westernmost of the four shorter avenues built on the swampy southeastern bulge of Manhattan and known as Alphabet City, in Crane's day an area populated primarily by poor immigrants packed into tenements.

The grind-organ says . . . Remember, remember
The cinder pile at the end of the backyard
Where we stoned the family of young
Garter snakes under . . .[14] And the monoplanes
We launched—with paper wings and twisted   20
Rubber bands[15] . . . Recall—recall

                                        the rapid tongues
That flittered from under the ash heap day
After day whenever your stick discovered
Some sunning inch of unsuspecting fibre—
It flashed back at your thrust, as clean as fire.[16]

And Rip was slowly made aware
    that he, Van Winkle, was not here

14. Crane's cinder pile is a desacralized version of the spirit-haunted spot described by Irving in the Postscript to "Rip van Winkle": "The favorite abode of this Manitou [Indian spirit] is still shown. It is a great rock or cliff in the loneliest part of the mountains. . . . Near the foot of it is a small lake . . . with water snakes basking in the sun on the leaves of the pond lilies which lie on the surface. This place was held in great awe by the Indians." Snakes figure elsewhere in *The Bridge* as symbols of time, eternity, and seductive femininity; here they belong to one of the personal memories triggered by the hurdy-gurdy. In connection with the deliberately Freudian recollections of the poet's parents developed below (see notes 19 and 20), the snakes may suggest a Medusa-like threat, which is reversed when the snakes are stoned instead of turning the onlooker to stone; that the underlying issue is possession of the phallus, the scepter of authority over cultural patrimony, becomes explicit in the subsequent description of the clash between the snakes' "sunning inch of . . . fibre" and the boy's prodding stick.

15. Irving's Rip made toys for the children in town and prompted their imaginations: "He assisted at their sports, made their playthings, taught them to fly kites and shoot marbles, and told them long stories of ghosts, witches, and Indians." Crane's toy monoplanes blindly prefigure the aerial dogfights of World War I, which figure prominently in "Cape Hatteras," but they also evoke the "barnstorming" spirit of early aviators and stunt pilots who traveled the country putting on air shows.

16. The snake here seems to hail from the poem by Emily Dickinson that Crane would have known as "A Narrow Fellow in the Grass" (number 1096 in R. W. Franklin's currently definitive edition). Unusually for her, Dickinson adopts the persona of a boy in this text to describe the "tighter breathing / And zero at the bone" prompted by encounters with the "spotted shaft": "Yet when a child, and barefoot, / I more than once, at morn, // Have passed, I thought, a whip-lash / Unbraiding in the sun,—" (I quote the poem in the over-edited form that would have been available to Crane; Dickinson's original reads: "But when a Boy and Barefoot / I more than once at Noon // Have passed I thought a Whip Lash / Unbraiding in the Sun.") As the image of the "rapid tongues" suggests, what is at stake for Crane in the memory is the question of who will inherit the power of a poetic speech capable of striking "clean as fire."

nor there.[17] *He woke and swore he'd seen Broadway*
a Catskill daisy chain in May—[18]

So memory, that strikes a rhyme out of a box,
Or splits a random smell of flowers through glass—
It is the whip stripped from the lilac tree   30
One day in spring my father took to me,[19]
Or is it the Sabbatical, unconscious smile
My mother almost brought me once from church[20]
And once only, as I recall—?

It flickered through the snow screen, blindly
It forsook her at the doorway, it was gone
Before I had left the window. It
Did not return with the kiss in the hall.

17. When Irving's Rip Van Winkle wakes up, he finds that, having slept through the American Revolution, he is, like Crane's version of him, neither "here" in the present nor "there" in the past: "There had been a revolutionary war . . . [so] that, instead of being a subject of his Majesty George the Third, he was now a free citizen of the United States."

18. Manhattan Island was urbanized slowly from its southern to its northern tip, a process not completed until late in the nineteenth century. When Crane's Van Winkle fell asleep, Lower Broadway was a meadow; when he wakes up, it is the thronged urban thoroughfare of modern New York.

19. Crane's personal recollections of his parents are shaped or chosen to carry a universalizing significance on the Freudian model, of which Crane was well aware. The father wields the phallic whip (a replica of Dickinson's whip-lash?) to interdict the blessing of the mother's smile, even though the smile is granted once only; the mother, in keeping with the Oedipal scenario, remains ultimately inaccessible, even rejecting, although within the framework of the poem she stands in the line of idealized maternal figures that includes Pocahontas, Queen Isabella, the Virgin Mary, and the pioneer mother of "Indiana." A similar idealization informs Irving's "Rip Van Winkle" (where, however, it counterpoints the misogynist image of the scolding wife): "The Kaatsberg or Catskill mountains have always been a region full of fable. The Indians considered them the abode of spirits who influenced the weather, spreading sunshine or clouds over the landscape and sending good or bad hunting seasons. They were ruled by an old squaw spirit, said to be their mother." That the father's whip is stripped from a lilac tree suggests an inversion of the idealized paternal relationship underwriting Whitman's elegy for Abraham Lincoln, "When Lilacs Last in the Dooryard Bloom'd"; Whitman breaks off a sprig of lilac, the symbol of "ever-returning spring," and leaves it in the dooryard in memory of the martyred president. The opening lines of Eliot's *The Waste Land*, "April is the cruelest month, / Breeding lilacs out of the dead land, / Mixing memory and desire," also hover in the background.

20. Crane told his mother, Grace Hart Crane, "My youth has been a rather bloody battleground for yours and father's sex life and troubles." Still, he sympathized with her so strongly that in 1917 he chose to call himself "Hart" rather than "Harold," his given name. The relationship soured permanently in 1928 after she threatened to tell his father about his homosexuality and tried to block a $5,000 inheritance left him by his grandmother. Crane was distracted from work on *The Bridge* by Grace's financial and emotional troubles; her letters often prompted his self-destructive drinking sprees.

Macadam, gun-grey as the tunny's belt,
Leaps from Far Rockaway to Golden Gate   40
Keep hold of that nickel for car-change, Rip,—[21]
Have you got your "*Times*"—?
And hurry along, Van Winkle—it's getting late![22]

21. Van Winkle is on his way to the subway. In "Cutty Sark," the phrase "somebody's nickel" suggests that Rip's coin has traveled too, from hand to hand.
22. An echo of the phrase " HURRY UP PLEASE IT'S TIME," which recurs throughout the pub scene concluding "A Game of Chess" in Eliot's *The Waste Land*.

3. Manhattan from the Bridge Tower, 1916.

THE RIVER

S tick your patent name on a signboard
brother—all over—going west—young man[1]
Tintex[2]—Japalac[3]—Certain-teed Overalls ads[4] . . .   . . . *and past*
and lands sakes! under the new playbill ripped   *the din and*
in the guaranteed corner—see Bert Williams what?[5]   *slogans of*

THE RIVER: In a letter Otto Kahn of September 27, 1927, Crane explains the transition from "Van Winkle" to "The River": "The subway is simply a figurative, psychological 'vehicle' for transporting the reader to the Middle West. He lands on the railroad tracks in the company of several tramps in the twilight. The extravagance of the first twenty-three lines of this section is an intentional burlesque on the cultural confusion of the present—a great conglomeration of noises analogous to the strident impression of a fast express running by. The rhythm is jazz." Slightly earlier, on July 4, he had written Mrs. T. W. Simpson: "I'm trying in this part of [*The Bridge*] to chart the pioneer experience of our forefathers—and to tell the story backwards, as it were, on the 'backs' of hobos. These hobos are simply 'psychological ponies' to carry the reader across the country and back to the Mississippi, which you will notice is described as a great River of Time. I also unlatch the door to the pure Indian world which opens out in 'The Dance' section, so the reader is gradually led back in time to the pure savage world, while existing at the same time in the present. It has been a very complicated thing to do, and I think I have worked harder and longer on this section of *The Bridge* than any other."

   1. "Go West, young man! Go West and grow up with the country" (usually abbreviated to its first four words) was a famous slogan in favor of Manifest Destiny coined or popularized by Horace Greeley in an editorial in the *New York Tribune* in 1865.

   2. Tintex: a brand of powder dye.

   3. Jap-a-lac: a combination stain-varnish for wooden furniture made in Cleveland by the Glidden Company.

   4. Certain-teed was a major manufacturer of building materials. The company, which is still in business, did not make overalls, but from 1925 through 1929 it ran a series of full-page, full-color ads drawn by Herbert Paus. Each ad depicted a brawny, bare-chested giant looming over a busy scene of industry or exploration; the latter included Columbus arriving in the New World, pioneers headed west in covered wagons or stage coaches, ships of various nations and eras in what looks like New York harbor, a sprawling rail yard, and a plane in flight against the background of the giant piloting a ship—all prominent themes in *The Bridge*. One of the ads even combines the New York skyline with an Eastern cityscape suggestive of Cathay. Several of the scenes of industry show workingmen in overalls, but it is hard to resist surmising that the allusion in the text, if not a simple mistake, is primarily a way to smuggle in the charismatic figure of the giant. At a minimum, Paus's drawings and Crane's poem share in, and show the power of, a system of national images once widely held in common. A selection of the ads may be viewed online at americanartarchivescom.comPaus_certainteed.htm.

   5. Bert Williams (1875–1922): an African-American singer, songwriter, and comedian, one of the preeminent entertainers of his day. After getting his start in vaudeville with blackface minstrel roles, he used his popularity to move beyond them and start clearing away "darkie" stereotypes from popular entertainment. In 1903, he starred in the first African-American musical to open on Broadway, *In Dahomey*.

Minstrels[6] when you steal a chicken just   *the year—*
save me the wing[7] for if it isn't
Erie[8] it ain't for miles around a
Mazda[9]—and the telegraphic night coming on[10] Thomas

a Ediford[11]—and whistling down the tracks   10
a headlight rushing with the sound—can you
imagine—while an EXPRESS makes time like
SCIENCE—COMMERCE and the HOLYGHOST
RADIO[12] ROARS IN EVERY HOME WE HAVE THE NORTHPOLE[13]
WALLSTREET AND VIRGINBIRTH WITHOUT STONES OR   15

6. Minstrel shows usually featured white actors in blackface masks or makeup and story-lines that exploited low-comic stereotypes about African Americans; an ancestor of vaudeville, minstrelsy was one of the most popular forms of entertainment in nineteenth-century America and had a significant afterlife in film comedy through the 1930s.

7. One of the most pervasive racist stereotypes of the first half of the twentieth century depicted African Americans as chicken thieves, supposedly because they were inordinately fond of fried chicken. The origins of the idea are a matter of dispute, but it was widely disseminated both in the minstrel shows of the nineteenth century and in early movies, including the Edison Company's *The Chicken Thieves* (1896) and Biograph's *The Chicken Thief* (1904). D. W. Griffith's 1915 epic *Birth of a Nation* contains an infamous scene in which black legislators in the Reconstruction South lounge with bare feet on their desks and eat fried chicken while seeking to pass laws legalizing interracial marriage ("miscegenation," in the racist jargon of the day).

8. The Erie Railroad, which ran from western New York State to Chicago.

9. A type of lamp manufactured by General Electric after 1909 for use with tungsten-filament light bulbs, which gave more light at lower cost than the carbon-filament bulbs previously in use. GE derived the name from the Zoroastrian deity Ahura-Mazda, the god of creation or light. The brand name was famous; the company continued the product line until shortly after the Second World War.

10. In the 1920s the telegraph had not yet been surpassed by the telephone as the primary means of transcontinental communication.

11. A conflation of the names of Thomas Edison and Henry Ford, prime architects of modernity with their inventions of the light bulb and phonograph, on the one hand, and the automobile assembly line, on the other. The names are further conflated with that of St. Thomas a Becket, the twelfth-century martyr (famously murdered in the cathedral at Canter-bury), whose shrine the pilgrims in Chaucer's *The Canterbury Tales* set out to visit, prefigur-ing the pilgrimage of Crane's hoboes.

12. "HOLYGHOST RADIO": the ambiguous syntax here is deliberate. The radio in general, its disembodied voice heard in every home, may replace the Holy Ghost, as science and com-merce replace Father and Son in the line "SCIENCE—COMMERCE and the HOLYGHOST." Or "HOLYGHOST RADIO" may refer in particular to the enormously popular broadcasts of such preachers as the politically engaged (and eventually proto-Fascist) Catholic priest Charles Coughlin, the fire-and-brimstone fundamentalist Bob Jones, Sr., and the Pentecostal revival-ist Aimee Semple McPherson, all of whom began their radio ministries in the 1920s.

13. In 1926, Admiral Richard E. Byrd claimed to have made the first flight over the North Pole; the feat was widely celebrated, but most polar historians now think the flight came short of its goal and may have been misrepresented by Byrd. Three days after Byrd's flight (in a three-engine plane), the Norwegian explorer Roald Amundson crossed the Pole in a dirigible.

WIRES OR EVEN RUNning brooks[14] connecting ears
and no more sermons windows flashing roar
breathtaking—as you like it . . . eh?

So the 20th Century—so
whizzed the Limited[15]—roared by and left
three men, still hungry on the tracks,[16] ploddingly   20
watching the tail lights wizen and converge, slip-
ping gimleted and neatly out of sight.[17]

* * * * * * * * * * *

The last bear, shot drinking in the Dakotas
Loped under wires that span the mountain stream.[18]
Keen instruments, strung to a vast precision
Blind town to town and dream to ticking dream.   *to those*
But some men take their liquor slow—and count   *whose*

14. Radio, the "wireless," transmits stock market reports, news of polar exploration, and
religious exhortation with equal and indifferent ease. The conjunction of sermons, stones,
and running brooks refers to Duke Senior's speech in act 2, scene 1 of Shakespeare's *As You
Like It* (whose title appears in vernacular two lines below). In the country, says the exiled
Duke, we can "Find tongues in trees, books in the running brooks, / Sermons in stones, and
good in everything."

15. "The 20th Century" is a pun on the era and on a famous train that symbolized its self-
conscious modernity. The train, the 20th Century Limited, was an elegant Pullman sleeper
running overnight between New York and Chicago; in the 1920s, Chicago, being a rail hub
(and the home of the Pullman Company), would have represented the gateway to the West.

16. The three men suggest a latter-day version of the biblical three Magi as hoboes; the
hoboes follow the taillights of the train as the Magi followed the star of Bethlehem. In the
1920s, the term *hobo* referred not to tramps in general but specifically to homeless migrants
who crisscrossed the country by "hopping freights"—stealing rides in boxcars as the trains
moved through the rail yards. In 1911, the *New York Telegraph* estimated the hobo population
of the country at 700,000; the numbers would increase dramatically during the Great
Depression.

17. The taillights converge as the train recedes into the distance; as the lights become
"gimleted," reduced to the size of one small circle, the scene closes in the manner of an iris
shot in early cinema. In a letter to Otto Kahn of September 12, 1927, Crane describes the
change that occurs in the poem after this caesura: "The rhythm settles down to a steady
pedestrian gait, like that of wanderers plodding along. My tramps are psychological vehicles,
also. Their wanderings as you will notice, carry the reader into interior after interior, finally
to the great River. They are the leftovers of the pioneers in at least this respect—that their
wanderings carry the reader through an experience parallel to that of Boone and others. I
think [I] have caught some of the essential spirit of the Great Valley here, and in the process
have approached the primal world of the Indian, which emerges with a full orchestra in the
succeeding dance."

18. Loping under wires carrying messages or electricity, the last bear is a victim of modernity and of the science and commerce that were making the wilderness disappear. Bears were
sacred to many of the Plains Indians of the Dakotas; the bear spirit was particularly important
in healing rituals.

—Though they'll confess no rosary nor clue— *addresses*
The river's minute by the far brook's year. *are never near*
Under a world of whistles, wires and steam
Caboose-like they go ruminating through
Ohio, Indiana—blind baggage—
To Cheyenne tagging . . . Maybe Kalamazoo.[19]

Time's rendings, time's blendings they construe
As final reckonings of fire and snow; 35
Strange bird-wit, like the elemental gist
Of unwalled winds they offer, singing low
My Old Kentucky Home[20] and *Casey Jones,*[21]
Some Sunny Day.[22] I heard a road-gang chanting so.
And afterwards, who had a colt's eyes—one said, 40

19. Compare Carl Sandburg's "Caboose Thoughts" (1918): "somehow and somewhere the end of the run / The train gets put together again / And the caboose and the green tail lights / Fade down the right of way like a new white hope" (ll. 12–15).

20. "My Old Kentucky Home" (1853), originally entitled "Poor Uncle Tom, Good Night," is a minstrel song by Stephen Foster about a former slave who longs for his old home in antebellum Kentucky: "The sun shines bright on my old Kentucky home; / 'Tis summer, the darkies are gay. / The corn top's ripe and the meadow's in bloom, / While the birds make music all the day." Often included in early dramatizations of Harriet Beecher Stowe's *Uncle Tom's Cabin,* the song, like many by Foster, acquired the status of virtual folk music. It was adopted as the state song of Kentucky in 1928; the state cleaned up the third line, replacing "darkies" with "people," in 1986.

21. Casey Jones (1863–1900): a train engineer who died heroically in a vain attempt to prevent the collision of a passenger train with a stopped freight on a foggy, rainy night in Vaughan, Mississippi (April 30, 1900). He became a folk hero after a friend, Wallace Saunders, an African American "engine wiper" (cleaner of steam engines) composed a ballad commemorating the tragedy to the tune of a popular song of the day, "Jimmie Jones." The song was popularized by Frank and Bert Leighton, vaudeville performers, whose brother, an engineer on the Illinois Central Railroad, had heard it and taught it to them. The first official version was published in 1909, crediting T. Lawrence Siebert with the lyrics and Eddie Newton with the music. The second verse of the original version bears most directly on *The Bridge*: "Caller called Jones about half-past four, / Jones kissed his wife at the station door, / Climbed into the cab with the orders in his hand, / Says "This is my trip to the promised land."

22. "Some Sunny Day," music and lyrics by Irving Berlin, 1922, is a nostalgic song about Alabama:

My heart goes pitter patter, no one knows what's the matter,
Just received a telegram from Alabam' my home.
That's why I'm gonna worry 'til the time when I hurry
Right back to that cabin door, never more to roam.
Some sunny day with a smile on my face
I'll go back to that place far away.

"Jesus! Oh I remember watermelon days!" [23] And sped
High on a cloud of merriment, recalled
"—And when my Aunt Sally Simpson smiled," he drawled—
"It was almost like Louisiana, long ago." [24]
"There's no place like Booneville though, Buddy,"   45
One said, excising a last burr from his vest,[25]
"—For early trouting." Then peering in the can,
"—But I kept on the tracks." Possessed, resigned,
He trod the fire down pensively and grinned,
Spreading dry shingles of a beard. . . .

                                Behind   50
My father's cannery works I used to see
Rail-squatters ranged in nomad raillery,[26]
The ancient men—wifeless or runaway
Hobo-trekkers that forever search
An empire wilderness of freight and rails.   55
Each seemed a child, like me, on a loose perch,
Holding to childhood like some termless play.
John, Jake or Charley, hopping the slow freight

23. "Watermelon days" suggests a time of holiday abundance in stark contrast to the hard life on the road gang. The lack of dialect suggests that the speaker is white, but the primary association of watermelon in Crane's America was with blacks, who were portrayed on postcards, on sheet-music covers, and in a surprising abundance of short films as avid eaters (and often thieves) of watermelons. Many of the films depicted watermelon-eating contests, which is the most likely referent here, independent of the troubling racial associations. Together with the allusions to "Some Sunny Day" and "My Old Kentucky Home," the line probably registers a nostalgia for the antebellum South, understood as a kind of lost Eden, that was common in American popular culture in the 1920s and 1930s and culminated in the almost immediate canonization of *Gone with the Wind* (both book and film).

24. A personal tribute. Sally Simpson was the elderly housekeeper of the Crane family cottage on the Isle of Pines, Cuba, where Crane worked on *The Bridge* in 1926. Crane regarded her as a surrogate mother; to his real mother, Grace, Crane wrote: "Mrs. Simpson lets me completely alone when I'm busy; lets me drum on the piano interminably if I want to—says she likes it—and she has assumed a tremendous interest in my poem." Aunt Sally came from New Orleans, which she recommended as a writer's retreat; Crane fell in love with the city after a brief visit there en route to New York.

25. To "live on the burr hole" was slang for "to be a drifter."

26. This passage reworks part of "The Fire Sermon" from Eliot's *The Waste Land*: "While I was fishing in the dull canal / On a winter evening round behind the gashouse / Musing upon the king my brother's wreck / And on the king my father's death before him." Eliot's allusion is to Shakespeare's *The Tempest*, whose Prince Ferdinand is, for the moment, like Crane's rail-squatters, homeless, even a kind of migrant laborer (Prospero puts him to work hauling logs). Crane's father owned a cannery in Warren, Ohio.

—Memphis to Tallahassee—riding the rods,
Blind fists of nothing, humpty-dumpty clods.[27]   60

Yet they touch something like a key perhaps.
From pole to pole across the hills, the states[28]
—They know a body under the wide rain;   *but who have*
Youngsters with eyes like fjords, old reprobates   *touched her,*
With racetrack jargon,—dotting immensity   *knowing her*
They lurk across her, knowing her yonder breast   *without name*
Snow-silvered, sumac-stained or smoky blue—
Is past the valley sleepers, south or west.[29]
—As I have trod the rumorous midnights, too,

And past the circuit of the lamp's thin flame   70
(O Nights that brought me to her body bare!)[30]

27. "Blind fists of nothing" may play on Eliot's "I will show you fear in a handful of dust," from the first section, "The Burial of the Dead," of *The Waste Land*; the dust becomes the "humpty-dumpty clods," which, like the egg in the nursery rhyme, "have a great fall" and cannot be "put together again." Crane's statement that the "hobo-trekkers . . . each seemed a child like me" is the key to the allusion. The hoboes hold onto memories of an idyllic childhood, in an earlier America, as a Romantic poet might do (the model is Wordsworth; compare Crane's "Passage": "In sapphire arenas of the hills / I was promised an improved infancy"); the memories form the "loose perch" from which the aspiring poet, like Humpty Dumpty, falls to earth and breaks. It is worth recalling that Lewis Carroll's Humpty Dumpty, in chapter 6 of *Through the Looking Glass*, has strong views about the power of language: "'When I use a word,' Humpty Dumpty said in rather a scornful tone, 'it means just what I choose it to mean — neither more nor less.' // 'The question is,' said Alice, 'whether you CAN make words mean so many different things.' // 'The question is,' said Humpty Dumpty, 'which is to be master—that's all.'"
28. Probably telegraph poles; perhaps boundary markers.
29. The bosom of the earth is, of course, proverbial, but the image of the hobo-trekkers "dotting immensity" may carry an echo of Baudelaire's "The Giantess" ("La Géante"):

> I would like to have lived by a young giantess . . .
> To roam at will her magnificent form,
> To scale the slopes of her enormous knees
> And sometimes in summer, when the oppressive sun
> Made her stretch out across the countryside,
> To sleep without cares in the shadow of her breast
> Like a peaceable hamlet beneath a mountainside.
>   (My translation)

30. These lines may derive from a passage in Section 21 of Whitman's *Song of Myself*:

> I am he that walks with the tender and growing night,
> I call to the earth and sea half-held by the night.
>
> Press close bare-bosom'd night—press close magnetic nourishing night!
> Night of south winds—night of the large few stars!
> Still nodding night—mad naked summer night.

Have dreamed beyond the print that bound her name.
Trains sounding the long blizzards out—I heard
Wail into distances I knew were hers.[31]
Papooses crying on the wind's long mane   75
Screamed redskin dynasties that fled the brain,
—Dead echoes! But I knew her body there,
Time like a serpent down her shoulder, dark,
And space, an eaglet's wing, laid on her hair.[32]

Under the Ozarks, domed by Iron Mountain,[33]   80
The old gods of the rain lie wrapped in pools
Where eyeless fish curvet a sunken fountain   *nor the*
And re-descend with corn from querulous crows.   *myths of her*
Such pilferings make up their timeless eatage,   *fathers . . .*
Propitiate them for their timber torn
By iron, iron—always the iron dealt cleavage![34]
They doze now, below axe and powder horn.[35]

31. These lines too, like much of the railroad imagery of "The River," are in dialogue with Whitman, in this case with "To a Locomotive in Winter":

> Type of the modern—emblem of motion and power—pulse of the continent—
> For once come serve the Muse and merge in verse, even as here I see thee,
> With storm and buffeting gusts of wind and falling snow;
> By day thy warning ringing bell to sound its notes,
> By night thy silent signal lamps to swing.
>
> Fierce-throated beauty!
> Roll through my chant with all thy lawless music, thy swinging lamps at night;
> Thy madly-whistled laughter, echoing, rumbling like an earthquake, rousing all.

32. The eagle and the serpent, symbolizing space and time, appear here together for the first time in *The Bridge*, prefiguring their prominent role in "The Dance." The symbolism derives primarily from Mesoamerican mythology, but it may also allude to Nietzsche's *Thus Spoke Zarathustra*, in which the eagle first appears at noon with a serpent coiled around its neck "not like prey, but like a friend" ("Zarathustra's Prologue," section 10). Zarathustra adopts the pair as "my animals" and ultimately takes them as confidants when he first formulates the idea of eternal recurrence.

33. Iron Mountain: a mountain in the Ozark range of southeastern Missouri, once thought to be made of solid iron. It was the site of extensive iron mining before the Civil War and one terminus of the Iron Mountain Railroad, which was built to deliver ore from Iron Mountain to St. Louis. The locale was made famous for a time by a folk ballad, "Iron Mountain Baby," recounting the (true) story of an infant rescued after being thrown from a train at Iron Mountain.

34. The iron cleavage is administered by the broad axe (mentioned in the next line) that cleared the forests, by the railroad ties that divided the land, and by the locomotives that traversed the continent; the steam locomotive was colloquially known as the iron horse.

35. Powder horn: a cow or buffalo horn hollowed out to carry gunpowder.

And Pullman breakfasters glide glistening steel[36]
From tunnel into field—iron strides the dew—
Straddles the hill, a dance of wheel on wheel.   90
You have a half-hour's wait at Siskiyou,
Or stay the night and take the next train through.
Southward, near Cairo passing, you can see
The Ohio merging,—borne down Tennessee;[37]
And if it's summer and the sun's in dusk   95
Maybe the breeze will lift the River's musk
—As though the waters breathed that you might know
Memphis Johnny,[38] *Steamboat Bill*,[39] *Missouri Joe*.[40]
Oh, lean from the window, if the train slows down,
As though you touched hands with some ancient clown,[41]   100

36. Pullman cars were luxury sleepers. The Pullman Company employed only African Americans as porters, a policy reflecting the racial theme, which is about to return to "The River" with renewed force.

37. The Ohio River is the largest tributary of the Mississippi, into which it flows near Cairo, Illinois.

38. Presumably a popular song, but otherwise unidentifiable. The place name, one of many that fill "The River," is probably more important than the song, whose title Crane may be either inventing or misremembering.

39. "Steamboat Bill": a popular ballad composed in 1910 by Bert Leighton to lyrics by Ren Shields. The song recounts the fatal misadventure of a riverboat captain told by his bosses to steam down the Mississippi and "beat the record of the *Robert E. Lee*"; the result is a catastrophic boiler explosion. The portions of the song most pertinent to "The River" are from the last verse and final chorus:

> There's crape on ev'ry steamboat that plows those streams,
> From Memphis right to Natchez down to New Orleans.
> The wife of Mister William was at home in bed
> When she got the telegram that Steamboat's dead.
> She said to the children "Bless each honey lamb,
> The next papa that you have will be a railroad man."
>
> . . . .
>
> Steamboat Bill, missing on the Mississippi,
> He's a pilot on a ferry in that Promised Land.

40. "Missouri Joe": a folklike ballad about the life and death of a gunslinging train robber, of origin unknown and now obscure; recorded by Sophie Tucker in 1911. (A video of the performance is available on YouTube.)

41. The "ancient clown" is impossible to identify with certainty. "Clown" seems to be used in its Elizabethan sense to mean a court jester, a "fool" dressed in motley who was given license to ridicule his nominal betters and remind them of uncomfortable truths. In this context, the clown may form a cross between two personae from the minstrel tradition, the low-comic stereotype of Zip Coon and the ennobled figure of Uncle Tom or Old Black Joe. The touching of hands (a metaphor for a meeting of gazes at a trestle over the Mississippi) represents a transient meeting between the white hoboes on the freight and their black counterparts on the river barges, who "hum *Deep River*" (see next note) as they head south.

—A little while gaze absently below
And hum *Deep River* with them while they go.[42]

Yes, turn again and sniff once more—look see,
O Sheriff, Brakeman and Authority—[43]
Hitch up your pants and crunch another quid,[44]   105
For you, too, feed the River timelessly.
And few evade full measure of their fate;
Always they smile out eerily what they seem.
I could believe he joked at heaven's gate—
Dan Midland—jolted from the cold brake-beam.[45]   110

Down, down[46]—born pioneers in time's despite,
Grimed tributaries to an ancient flow—
They win no frontier by their wayward plight,
But drift in stillness, as from Jordan's brow.[47]

You will not hear it as the sea; even stone   115
Is not more hushed by gravity . . . But slow,
As loth to take more tribute—sliding prone
Like one whose eyes were buried long ago

The River, spreading, flows—and spends your dream.[48]
What are you, lost within this tideless spell?   120

42. "Deep River": a Negro Spiritual of unknown origin, composed before 1875 and popularized by the Fisk Jubilee Singers. The lyrics to its chorus are "Deep river, / My home is
over Jordan, / Deep river, Lord, / I want to [later: I'm gonna] cross over into camp ground."
Crossing the river symbolized both entry into the Promised Land after death and escape from
slavery. Fugitive slaves on the Underground Railroad crossed the Ohio River, the border
between free and slave territory, from Kentucky into Ohio near Cincinnati.

43. This less than holy trinity is representative of the hardened "bulls" who patrolled the
rail yards in legendary conflict with the hoboes.

44. Quid: a plug of chewing tobacco.

45. A legendary hobo who died hopping a freight.

46. "Down, down": movement south along the Mississippi River. The focus at this point
shifts from the white hoboes to the black men who work on the water; the latter are the
"grimed tributaries," "grimed" suggesting the both the grime of toil and (recalling the tradition of blackface) the color of the men's skin. Like the pioneers who headed west, these men
are "wayward," but their plight, the legacy of slavery and Jim Crow, denies them a frontier
to conquer; their movement is toward the sea that brought their ancestors to the New World
in chains.

47. Still unfree, the descendants of slaves drift on the Mississippi, figuratively unable to
cross the Jordan into the Promised Land.

48. "The River, spreading, flows": the spreading forms the Mississippi River Delta in the
heart of the slave South, including New Orleans, from which the river empties into the sea.

You are your father's father,[49] and the stream—
A liquid theme that floating niggers swell.[50]

Damp tonnage and alluvial march of days—
Nights turbid, vascular with silted shale
And roots surrendered down of moraine clays:[51]   125
The Mississippi drinks the farthest dale.[52]

O quarrying passion, undertowed sunlight!
The basalt surface drags a jungle grace
Ochreous and lynx-barred in lengthening might;
Patience! and you shall reach the biding place!   130

Over De Soto's bones the freighted floors[53]
Throb past the City storied of three thrones.[54]

49. Despite the resemblance, this is probably not an allusion to Wordsworth's famous line "The child is father of the man" ("My Heart Leaps Up"). The "you" here addresses both the black boatmen and the readers drawn (like the passing hoboes earlier) into momentary alliance with them. In the 1920s. the father's fathers of these men would have been slaves, and within the "tideless swell" of the river—the legendary Father of Waters—their descendants reenact the fate of their forefathers.

50. Crane's use of the infamous racial epithet is an embarrassment today, but it would not have raised many eyebrows in the mid 1920s. The reference (which intends to be sympathetic) is to the work songs that black stevedores and bargemen inherited from their slave ancestors. A similar usage occurs in another portrait of river life written, like "The River," in 1927, the musical Show Boat, with music by Jerome Kern and lyrics by Oscar Hammerstein. The verse of the signature song, "Ol' Man River," began with the lines (altered for the better by Paul Robeson in 1936 and rarely used since) "Niggers all work on de Mississippi, / Niggers all work while de white folks play." The treatment of the river in the song is strikingly similar to Crane's treatment of it as "a great River of time"; the musical premiered in December, however, months after the poem was finished.

51. Moraine: a mass of rocks and sediment deposited by a glacier.

52. The Mississippi "drinks the furthest dale" because it is fed by so many tributaries. As the meeting point of the continent's major waterways, the river (the "great River of time") becomes all-encompassing in its journey toward the sea, the "biding place" in which the dreaming river, "tortured by history," seeks release. But the destination is equivocal: the river meets the Gulf of Mexico with hosannas, albeit silent ones, but the sea is "stinging": Matthew Arnold's "Unplumbed, salt, estranging sea" ("To Marguerite"), its sting here perhaps touched by a memory of the slave overseer's whip.

53. Hernando De Soto: conquistador and explorer. In 1541 De Soto led an expedition that crossed the Mississippi, which he claimed to be the first European to see, and proceeded west across the Ozarks. The explorers were seeking gold, silver, and other treasure, and, like Columbus, a route to Cathay. They returned with none of them—and without De Soto, who died on the western banks of the Mississippi in 1542. De Soto had sought to make the Indians of the region believe he was an immortal sun god; trying, without much success, to uphold the myth, his men hid his body in blankets weighted with sand and sunk the shroud in the river during the night. Hence the "freighted floors" (that is, barges) on the river steam over De Soto's bones.

54. New Orleans, the successive property of France, Spain, and France again, before being sold to the United States in the Louisiana Purchase of 1803.

Down two more turns the Mississippi pours
(Anon tall ironsides up from salt lagoons)[55]

And flows within itself, heaps itself free.[56]   135
All fades but one thin skyline 'round . . .Ahead
No embrace opens but the stinging sea;
The River lifts itself from its long bed,

Poised wholly on its dream, a mustard glow
Tortured with history, its one will—flow!   140
—The Passion spreads in wide tongues, choked and slow,[57]
Meeting the Gulf, hosannas silently below.[58]

55. Ironsides: ironclad warships from the Civil War, apparently once sunken and now dredged up. New Orleans is surrounded by coastal lagoons, including Lake Pontchartrain.

56. The river backs up and flows out into the delta.

57. The Passion: both the suffering and crucifixion of Christ and the ceremonies and musical compositions (most famously Bach's *St. Matthew Passion*) that commemorate it. Here the commemoration, merging with the text of the poem, "spreads in wide tongues," that is, in the poet's charismatic and prophetic utterance. There may be an echo here of Shelley's "Ode to the West Wind": "And, by the incantation of this verse, // Scatter, as from an unextinguish'd hearth / Ashes and sparks, my words among mankind!" The incantation is "choked and slow" in keeping with the flow of the river.

58. "Hosannas" here is a verb meaning "rejoices," continuing the religious figuration started with "The Passion" and resonant with the imperative "hosanna" in the *Sanctus* and *Benedictus* of the Catholic Mass.

THE DANCE

The swift red flesh, a winter king[1]—
Who squired the glacier woman down the sky?[2]

Then you shall
see her truly

THE DANCE: In a letter to Otto Kahn, Crane wrote of "The Dance": "Here one is on the pure mythical and smoky soil at last! Not only do I describe the conflict between the two races in this dance—I also become identified with the Indian and his world before it is over, which is the only method of ever really possessing the Indian and his world as a cultural factor. I think I really succeed in getting under the skin of this glorious and dying animal, and in terms of expression in symbols which he, himself, would comprehend. Pocahontas (the continent) is the common basis of our meeting; she survives the extinction of the Indian who finally, after being assumed into the elements of nature (as he understood them) persists only as a kind of 'eye' in the sky, or as a star that hangs between day and night—'the twilight's dim perpetual throne'" (September 12, 1927). Crane's comments reiterate the idea, still widespread in the 1920s, that "the Indian"—a catchall category indifferent to distinctions of culture, geography, and history—was a vanishing breed, destined to survive only in the cultural memory of its conquerors. Among the many possible sources for this idea is *Our America* (1919), by Crane's friend Waldo Frank: "The Indian is dying and is doomed. There can be no question of this. There need be no sentimentality. It may seem unjust that a spiritual culture as fine as this should be blotted out. . . . But Justice is an anthropomorphic fantasy. . . . The white man came with his material prowess, and under the steel hail of his onslaught the world of the Indian, its profound residence in nature, lies maimed and buried. No one knows this better, meets this more fearlessly, than the Indian himself." In voicing its similar conception, "The Dance" freely conflates three very different Indian peoples: the Aztecs, already long "extinct," the Algonquin confederation of the east coast of North America, and the Indians of the Great Plains. Assimilation and the attenuation of tribal identity had long been federal policy, administered by the Bureau of Indian Affairs, although a vigorous reform movement had developed by the mid 1920s.

1. The winter king is a composite figure, probably modeled in part on the Aztec god Quetzalcoatl, who was, among other things, the creator of books and the calendar, the giver of maize, the patron of priests, and the Morning Star (hence Crane's "'eye' in the sky"); the maize and the star intimate Quetzalcoatl's identity (though he is never named) and introduce the motif of death and rebirth in the cycle of nature, which comports with the iconic representation of Quetzalcoatl as a feathered serpent. In this connection, the presiding figure of Crane's text exemplifies the dying and reviving gods basic to all world religions according to Sir James George Frazer's influential study of comparative religion, *The Golden Bough* (first published 1890, expanded edition 1912), which Crane had studied intensively. Frazer's core scenario provides the basic armature of "The Dance": the god, usually a solar figure, unites in a mystic marriage with a fertility goddess, usually identified with grain or maize; the god or a human surrogate undergoes violent death or sacrifice in autumn followed by regeneration in spring; his death plunges the goddess into mourning, which leaves the earth itself in the grip of wintry death. Variations on this basic narrative are, of course, numerous (so much so that most modern scholars discredit Frazer's claim of a unitary original). The story of Quetzalcoatl's death and rebirth begins with a sexual transgression: a trickster god gets him drunk and lures him into sleeping with a celibate priestess, in some accounts his own sister. Remorseful, he leaves the city he has ruled, travels to the sea, immolates himself, and rises up as the Morning Star, which Crane prefers to the sun as a presiding symbol. Another version of the story identifies the star with Quetzalcoatl's heart; there are numerous variants, all of them representing a conflation of mythological imagery with the historical memory of the Toltec prophet-king who was Quetzalcoatl's namesake and template.

2. The glacier woman is probably the mountain Ixaccíhuatl, whose name means "White Woman"; Ixaccíhuatl has four peaks with permanent snow cover, corresponding to the head,

She ran the neighing canyons all the spring;
She spouted arms; she rose with maize—to die.[3]

And in the autumn drouth,[4] whose burnished hands
With mineral wariness found out the stone
Where prayers, forgotten, streamed the mesa sands?[5]
He holds the twilight's dim, perpetual throne.[6]

Mythical brows we saw retiring—loth,
Disturbed and destined, into denser green.
Greeting they sped us, on the arrow's oath:
Now lie incorrigibly what years between . . .

—your blood
remembering
its first
invasion of
her secrecy,
its first encounters
with her kin,
her chieftain
lover . . . his
shade that
haunts the
lakes and hills

chest, knees, and feet of a sleeping woman. Aztec myth regards this mountain as the metamorphosed form of a tragic lover, paired with her beloved in the form of the adjacent volcano Popocatétl, which is mentioned in "Cutty Sark." Crane's glacier woman recalls the avatar of Pocahontas who presides over the wintry scene of "The Harbor Dawn" and whose presence fades along with the morning star as that poem ends. In "The Dance" the winter king in effect reawakens the White Woman and "squires" her into spring as Pocahontas.

3. Rising with the maize, Pocahontas fuses with the mother goddesses surveyed by Frazer, who offers evidence that associations between the fertility goddess and corn (maize) are abundant worldwide. *The Golden Bough* documents the worship of the Corn Mother among both the Aztecs and the "Eastern Indians of North America." Like the classical Demeter (Roman Ceres), Crane's Pocahontas presides over the agricultural cycle and brings life each year to the dead land (associated with the absence of Demeter's daughter Persephone, who must unwillingly spend half the year as queen of the underworld). Crane's use of these myths forms part of his running dialogue with Eliot's *The Waste Land*, to which *The Bridge* forms a New World counterstatement.

4. In the context of *The Golden Bough*, the autumn drought corresponds to the annual death of the god and the corresponding death of the earth after the harvest. Crane here personifies the latter by fusing Pocahontas with a Persephone-like figure: "She spouted arms; she rose with maize—to die."

5. Images of Quetzalcoatl were carved in stone on the walls of Aztec temples. The prayers that once streamed out during the associated rituals are forgotten because the culture that gave rise to them is extinct.

6. "He": Quetzalcoatl as the Morning Star. The throne of the morning twilight is dim because the European conquest of the New World has destroyed the world of "the Indian" with its "profound residence in nature" (Waldo Frank; see the headnote to this poem). As the next two lines explain, the reluctant ("loth," that is, loath) mythical brows of the god have "retired" in defeat: they have either withdrawn into demythologized forms, exemplified by the "denser" (more opaque) green of a nature "disturbed" by modern consciousness and "the white man's technical prowess," or they have receded into the denser (thicker) green of the "incorrigibly" distant past.

There was a bed of leaves, and broken play;[7]
There was a veil upon you, Pocahontas, bride—
O princess whose brown lap was virgin May;
And bridal flanks and eyes hid tawny pride.

I left the village for dogwood.[8] By the canoe   17
Tugging below the mill-race, I could see
Your hair's keen crescent running, and the blue
First moth of evening take wing stealthily.

What laughing chains the water wove and threw![9]
I learned to catch the trout's moon whisper; I
Drifted how many hours I never knew
But, watching, saw that fleet young crescent die,—[10]

And one star, swinging, take its place, alone,   25
Cupped in the larches of the mountain pass—

7. Pocahontas's play is "broken" because she was only ten years old in 1607 old when, according to legend (assumed by Crane as fact), she intervened to save the captive John Smith from execution by a group of her father's hunters; the epigraph to "Powhatan's Daughter" describes her girlish frolics. "Pocahontas" is actually a childhood nickname, roughly meaning "little wanton." Pocahontas's youth facilitates the transition to her as a veiled, that is, virgin, bride in the next line (compare the veil of fog in "The Harbor Dawn") and to the Virgin Mary in the line after that. The trope of virginity refers both to the American continent as virgin land and to the eventual name of the colony, Virginia, appropriated from Pocahontas and her people, a theme resumed in "Virginia," the last of "Three Songs." May is Mary's month in the Catholic calendar; as an epithet for Pocahontas, "virgin May" reaffirms her association with the spring rebirth of growing things, fusing the image of the corn mother with the Virgin mother who was, in effect, Columbus's Pocahontas in "Ave Maria."

8. This line initiates the speaker's identification with Pocahontas's chieftain lover, although the two personae do not become distinct until late in the poem and never cease their alternate fusion and separation. Crane explained that he was attempting "an identification of myself (or reader) for the moment with the Indian savage while he is in the process of absorption into the elements of the pure nature-world around him" (To Yvor Winters, June 4, 1930).

9. The "laughing chains" of the river recall the "chained bay waters" of "To Brooklyn Bridge," into which, across the span of tragic history, they will decline; the Bridge, with its "choiring strings" and "bound cable strands," is supposed to reverse the process by becoming "our" modern myth, woven and thrown across the waters.

10. The crescent of the river freshet, representing Pocahontas's hair above, becomes the setting crescent moon, another image of the attenuation, but also the elegiac preservation, of the Indians' presence on the continent.

Until, immortally, it bled into the dawn.[11]
I left my sleek boat nibbling margin grass . . .[12]

I took the portage climb, then chose
A further valley-shed; I could not stop.
Feet nozzled wat'ry webs of upper flows;
One white veil gusted from the very top.

O Appalachian Spring![13] I gained the ledge; 33
Steep, inaccessible smile that eastward bends
And northward reaches in that violet wedge
Of Adirondacks![14]—wisped of azure wands,

Over how many bluffs, tarns, streams I sped!
—And knew myself within some boding shade:—[15]
Grey tepees tufting the blue knolls ahead,[16]
Smoke swirling through the yellow chestnut glade . . .

A distant cloud, a thunder-bud—it grew, 41
That blanket of the skies: the padded foot

11. The moon gives way to the Morning Star, once again an image and trace of Quetzal-coatl, transfigured by sacrifice and bleeding immortally into dawn. The image may also have a more general resonance. The morning star is a revered figure in the mythology of the Plains Indians, associated with life, strength, and fertility, and with the red-fleshed figure of a strong man adorned with an eagle's feather.

12. The passage from water to land, east to west, and low to high elevation recapitulates the direction of history as the poem conceives it.

13. A misreading of this exclamation provided Aaron Copland and Martha Graham with the title of their famous ballet of 1942, which also centers on a symbolic marriage; the "spring" of the ballet is the season, that of the poem a wellhead.

14. The northern turn of the chieftain/poet extends the geographic scope of Pocahontas's union with her chieftain lover to embrace the full sweep of the North American coastal lands inhabited by the Algonquin confederation, the Indian nation to which Pocahontas belonged, within the borders of what would become the United States.

15. After journeying deep into the mountains, the speaker arrives at an Indian village. The journey can be read as an inversion of its counterpart in Eliot's "What the Thunder Said," which proceeds through barren rocks to a "decayed hole among the mountains" before the thunder breaks and brings rain; Pocahontas's chieftain lover moves through a landscape rich in color and water to receive the flowering of the "thunder-bud," both a rain cloud and Pocahontas's virginity.

16. The Algonquins lived in wigwams (or wetus; circular wooden frames covered with woven mats and birch bark) not teepees (conical wooden frames covered in buffalo hide), which formed the dwellings of the Plains Indians.

Within,[17]—I heard it; 'til its rhythm drew,
—Siphoned the black pool from the heart's hot root!

A cyclone threshes in the turbine crest,
Swooping in eagle feathers down your back;[18]
Know, Maquokeeta,[19] greeting; know death's best;
—Fall, Sachem, strictly as the tamarack![20]

A birch kneels. All her whistling fingers fly.   49
The oak grove circles in a crash of leaves;
The long moan of a dance is in the sky.
Dance, Maquokeeta: Pocahontas grieves . . .

17. The beat of the padded, that is, moccasined, foot "within" the approaching thunder cloud fuses the storm with the wedding dance; it is impossible to say which one is the metaphor for the other. The dance is also a dance of death, as the emptying of the laden storm cloud's "black pool" becomes the spilling of the heart's blood. The death of the chieftain, which prepares his rebirth, takes multiple forms in what follows but ultimately merges with the immolation and metamorphosis of Quetzalcoatl.

18. The dance moves like both a cyclone and, anachronistically, a turbine, undulating with the eagle feathers of the chieftain's headdress. Quoting these two lines in a letter, Crane noted "the currency of Indian symbolism in whatever is most real in our little native culture." He continues: "I may exaggerate, but why did I really *have* to employ mention of the turbine engine to really describe the warrior's head-dress? Etc. Of course the head could have been elaborated in prose, but the psychic factor would have been lost via a delayed delivery. Our metaphysical preference for condensation, density—has a correspondence, an intense one, in the very elements of Indian design and ritual" (to Yvor Winters, November 15, 1926). The headdress of eagle feathers, the war bonnet beloved of Hollywood, was worn only by Plains Indians; Algonquin headgear did not resemble it. Crane needs the eagle feathers to repeat his identification, established in "The River," of the eagle with space and the serpent with time; the two symbols combine here in the figures of the plumed serpent Quetzalcoatl and his later Algonquin avatar, the chieftain Maquokeeta, who is named in the next line.

19. Named for the first time, the chieftain is either summoned to know that, for him, death is best or to receive "death's best," that is, the best of death or best death, the sacrificial-historical immolation that will grant him transfiguration and (a term introduced in the concluding passage) "freedom," presumably freedom from history itself. Crane told Yvor Winters that he had appropriated the name *Maquokeeta* from a New York City taxi driver, "obviously of Indian extraction (and a splendid fire-drinker)"; this unlikely native informant had told Crane, probably his lover for the evening, that his "Indian name" was Maquokeeta. Crane asked Winters if the latter could authenticate the name and then, when that proved impossible, decided that evocative vagueness was preferable. A letter of doubtful authority (discussed by Gordon A. Tapper in *The Machine That Sings*) claims that the taxi driver glossed the name as "big river."

20. Sachem: a North American Indian chief, especially of the Algonquins. Tamarack: an American larch tree. The word is Algonquian; the tree's reddish brown bark may have suggested to Crane the "swift red flesh" of the (felled) chieftain / winter king; the sachem's fall is as "strict," that is, inevitable or inexorable, as the clearing of the land. A conifer, the tamarack reproduces by dropping its cones, which may give another sense to "Fall, Sachem" and intimate yet again the cycle of death and rebirth.

And every tendon scurries toward the twangs
Of lightning deltaed down your saber hair.[21]
Now snaps the flint in every tooth; red fangs
And splay tongues thinly busy the blue air . . .

Dance, Maquokeeta! snake that lives before,   57
That casts his pelt, and lives beyond![22] Sprout, horn!
Spark, tooth![23] Medicine-man, relent, restore—
Lie to us,[24]—dance us back to the tribal morn!

Spears and assemblies: black drums thrusting on—
O yelling battlements,—I, too, was liege
To rainbows currying each pulsant bone:
Surpassed the circumstance, danced out the siege![25]

21. The flash of lightning pulsates through the dance, figuratively electrifying Maquokeeta's limbs—an idea that will return below.

22. The address to Maquokeeta as a snake, picking up on the images of fangs and splay tongues from the previous stanza, completes the chieftain's identification with the plumed serpent Quetzalcoatl begun by the earlier mention of the eagle feathers in the undulating headdress. The snake's shedding of its skin is a traditional symbol of rebirth.

23. The injunction "Spark, tooth!" echoes the previous stanza's "Now snaps the flint in every tooth"; the snapping of the flint yields the spark, intimating the start of the chieftain/Quetzalcoatl's immolation; the subsequent "Lie to us,—dance us back to the tribal morn" alludes yet again to the Morning Star, which "lives beyond" the shedding or burning off of the serpent's skin. The "tooth" is a little puzzling, but taken with the image of the splay tongues it may suggest an oral force that translates into the utterance of the poem.

24. Crane glossed "Lie to us" by observing that "All I am saying amounts in substance to this: 'Mimic the scene of yesterday; I want to see how it looked'" (to Yvor Winters, June 4, 1930).

25. This stanza may conflate the chieftain's/speaker's ordeal with Aztec rituals of human sacrifice, returning to the "tribal morn" in its most primitive or archaic form. The Aztec gods were thought to sustain human life by continually sacrificing their own blood and body parts; human sacrifice in kind was one of the bases of Mesoamerican culture. The poem's earlier images of snapping flint and the heart's hot root play into this theme. The most common form of Aztec sacrifice involved laying the victim out on a slab, piercing his or her abdomen with a flint knife, and extracting the still-beating heart from the body ("currying the pulsant bone")—all before an audience (the "yelling battlements"), whose members imitatively stabbed at themselves while singing and dancing to percussive music. The speaker's "I, too, was liege" reiterates his identification with the agonized/ecstatic Maquokeeta, whose body pulsates to the "twangs" of the lightning and the drums of the thunder.

And buzzard-circleted, screamed from the stake;[26]   65
I could not pick the arrows from my side.[27]
Wrapped in that fire, I saw more escorts wake—[28]
Flickering, sprint up the hill groins like a tide.

I heard the hush of lava wrestling your arms,
And stag teeth foam about the raven throat;[29]
Flame cataracts of heaven in seething swarms
Fed down your anklets to the sunset's moat.

O, like the lizard in the furious noon,   73
That drops his legs and colors in the sun,
—And laughs, pure serpent, Time itself, and moon
Of his own fate, I saw thy change begun![30]

26. The stake initially suggests burning, with overtones of Christian martyrdom, an idea developed by "Wrapped in that fire" in the line after next; the fire as wrapping is a shroud or cocoon from which the reborn chieftain/god arises, like Quetzalcoatl, in a new form. North American Indians did use burning as a form of execution (more often by protracted exposure than by conflagration), but Crane's source here is probably more literary than historical; in James Fennimore Cooper's *The Last of the Mohicans* (1826), the titular hero, Uncas, who, like Maquokeeta, embodies an ancient lineage, is condemned to be burned at the stake by the Hurons. (In the end, he dies from a stab in the back, but like Maquokeeta's, his death bears the mark of tragic inevitability.) For a different layer of allusion, see the next note.

27. The martyr's side pierced by arrows suggests the iconography of St. Sebastian. Tied to a stake and "hedgehogged" by Roman arrows (ca. 288 BCE), Sebastian should have died from his wounds but miraculously survived; his de facto resurrection allowed him to be martyred a second time. The allusion to Christianity is not as remote as it may seem; part of Frazer's project in *The Golden Bough* was to assimilate Christian narratives and rituals into his master plot of cyclical death and rebirth. St. Sebastian was also a favorite icon of homosexual desire, which may act as a subtext to the speaker's absorption with Maquokeeta.

28. The "escorts" appear to be other dancers who figuratively catch fire around Maquokeeta. The fire that consumes the chieftain/god may itself be figurative, the self-consuming energy of Maquokeeta's dance; the implication would be that he immolates himself by dancing himself to death. Several of the next stanza's metaphors for his movements —the lava in the arms, the "flame cataracts of heaven," the sunset's moat—suggest as much. The dance as fire would comport with the earlier identification of the dance as rainstorm by adding lightning to thunder, an association reaffirmed in the later line "Thewed of the levin," that is, of the lightning, "thunder-shod and lean."

29. The stag teeth presumably dangle from an ornamental necklace that undulates as Maquokeeta dances.

30. Another reiteration of the associations between time, the shedding of reptile skin, and the metamorphosis of the self-immolated god into the Morning Star, now beginning to prefigure a new phase of history marked by the extinction of "the Indian" and his "purely natural" world.

And saw thee dive to kiss that destiny
Like one white meteor,[31] sacrosanct and blent
At last with all that's consummate and free
There, where the first and last gods keep thy tent.

* * *

Thewed of the levin, thunder-shod and lean,[32]
Lo, through what infinite seasons dost thou gaze—
Across what bivouacs of thine angered slain,
And see'st thy bride immortal in the maize![33]

Totem and fire-gall, slumbering pyramid—[34]
Though other calendars now stack the sky,[35]
Thy freedom is her largesse, Prince, and hid
On paths thou knewest best to claim her by.

---

31. The white meteor may be thought of as a falling star, a form that, like Maquokeeta, shines brightest as it disappears in flames. The equation of the meteor with the chieftain's sacrificial destiny may also allude to a comet seen in Mexico in 1517 at about the same time the Aztec emperor Moctezuma II first received word that the Spanish had landed on the continent; the comet was taken to portend the fall of Aztec civilization, which followed swiftly under Hernan Cortés, from 1519 to 1521. Moctezuma was also long said to understand the comet as portending the second coming of Quetzalcoatl, though most historians now doubt the story. Another portent observed about the same time was a pyramidal sheet of fire in the east, which may correspond to the "flame cataracts of heaven" that seem to run down Maquokeeta's legs. After *The Bridge* was published, Crane planned an epic poem about Moctezuma and Cortés. In 1931, with a Guggenheim fellowship, he traveled to Mexico to write the new work; its abject failure probably contributed to his suicide

32. "Thewed of the levin": sinewed by lightning. "Thunder-shod" echoes the earlier "padded foot within" the thunder. "Lean" is hard to make sense of, as are many of the details in "The Dance"; it is as if the poem were performing a verbal self-immolation to match the ritual immolation of Maquokeeta's dance.

33. At this point Maquokeeta has assumed his transfigured form and unites with his bride by gazing at the maize from the sky. Their union supposedly overrides the history of violence against the "angered slain," a concession that comports with Crane's, and Waldo Frank's, notion that "the Indian" fearlessly embraced the necessity of disappearing. The result, evoked in the subsequent stanzas, is a transcendental freedom for "the Indian" and the flowering of both the North and South American continents into a fecund incarnation of the eternally virgin Pocahontas.

34. The three epithets of this line reiterate the sacrificial dimension of Maquokeeta's transfiguration: he is a totem (thought of, following Frazer, as a sacred animal that may be killed and eaten only on "rare and solemn occasions," usually annual rituals); he is a gall, an open wound rubbed raw, composed of fire (with additional significations of bitterness and bile); and he is the incarnation of a lost civilization (Aztec pyramids housed temples where human sacrifice was practiced; the pyramid at Cholula was sacred to Quetzalcoatl, who was depicted there with a flaming miter on his head).

35. The "calendars" are probably modern buildings like the skyscrapers of Crane's Manhattan, the architecture of a world that measures time by the Roman calendar.

High unto Labrador the sun strikes free   89
Her speechless dream of snow,[36] and stirred again,
She is the torrent and the singing tree;
And she is virgin to the last of men . . .

West, west and south! winds over Cumberland
And winds across the llano grass resume[37]
Her hair's warm sibilance. Her breasts are fanned
O stream by slope and vineyard—into bloom!

And when the caribou slant down for salt   97
Do arrows thirst and leap? Do antlers shine
Alert, star-triggered in the listening vault
Of dusk?[38]—and are her perfect brows to thine?

We danced, O Brave, we danced beyond their farms,
In cobalt desert closures made our vows . . .
Now is the strong prayer folded in thine arms,
The serpent with the eagle in the boughs.[39]

---

36. The snows of Labrador form a northern counterpart to the glacier woman Ixaccíhuatl, initiating a sweeping geographical movement developed in the next two stanzas.

37. The sweep continues westward, toward the Cumberland Mountains (inland from Pocahontas's Tidewater) and southward toward South America, with its broad, treeless plains of llano grass.

38. The image of the shining antlers of the caribou at a salt lick recall the "stag's teeth" that quiver as Maquokeeta dances; in its conjunction with the poem's final allusion to the chieftain/god as the Morning Star, the image reiterates the identification of Maquokeeta as a totem animal sacrificed in a solemn ritual—not annual, but epochal. The caribou, an arctic or subarctic species of reindeer, further extends the geographical sweep of the poem's closing passage.

39. The union of the eagle and the serpent, glossed by Crane in "The River" as the reconciliation of space and time, also marks the reconciliation of myth and history that is the fundamental project of *The Bridge*. As observed in the notes to "The River," the image derives in part from Nietzsche's *Thus Spoke Zarathustra*; it also plays an important role in Shelley's *Laon and Cynthia; or, the Revolt of Islam*. But the principal model, which the poem seeks symbolically to recapitulate, is probably the legend of the founding of the Aztec capital of Tenochtitlan. In the version that Crane would have known, the Mexicans were enjoined to build their city at the spot where they would find an eagle on a prickly pear cactus devouring a serpent. (The original sources actually disagree on what, if anything, the eagle had in its beak.) The image became the basis for the coat of arms of modern Mexico; its relationship to the founding of a nation and a civilization—not to mention its resemblance to the Great Seal of the United States, where the eagle, with a sheaf of arrows in one talon and a sheaf of wheat in the other, grasps a serpentine banner in its beak bearing the legend "e pluribus unum"—allows for a seamless assimilation to the founding of a new America. The Bridge, the mythic center of this new New World, spanning the harbor of its mythic city, both soars like the eagle and curves like the serpent.

INDIANA

The morning glory, climbing the morning long   *. . . and read*
Over the lintel on its wiry vine,   *her in a*
Closes before the dusk, furls in its song   *mother's*
    As I close mine . . .[1]   *farewell gaze.*

And the bison thunder rends my dreams no more[2]
    As once my womb was torn, my boy, when you
Yielded your first cry at the prairie's door . . .
        Your father knew

Then, though we'd buried him behind us, far   9
    Back on the gold trail—then his lost bones stirred. . . .
But you who drop the scythe to grasp the oar
        Knew not, nor heard

INDIANA: According to Crane, this poem was planned as "the monologue of an Indiana farmer; time, about 1860. He has failed in the gold-rush and is returned to till the soil. His monologue is a farewell to his son, who is leaving for a life on the sea. It is a lyrical summary of the period of conquest, and his wife, the mother who died on the way back from the gold-rush, is alluded to in a way which implies her succession to the nature-symbolism of Pocahontas" (to Otto Kahn, September 12, 1927). In the final version, the monologue belongs to the mother, and the father has died on the gold trail before the birth of his son. The gold rush is the largest in American history, the Colorado or Pike's Peak gold rush of 1858 to 1861. Exemplified by the once-famous phrase "Pike's Peak or bust!" it drew a massive tide of miners and settlers to the Rocky Mountains. One consequence was that the Indian tribes of northern Colorado found their traditional way of life disintegrating as new trails and settlers encroached on Indian lands and poached their game. A displaced Indian women plays the pivotal role in Crane's text.

1. John T. Irwin suggests that "Indiana" alludes to a popular song, "the 1917 ballad 'Indiana,' perhaps better known by its first line as 'Back Home Again in Indiana,' with its imagery of nostalgic longing for a rural, childhood home: 'The new mown hay sends all its fragrance / From the fields I used to roam, / When I dream about the moonlight on the Wabash, / Then I long for my Indiana home,' as if the twentieth-century ballad expressed the feelings of the runaway son grown older."

2. "Bison thunder": the hoof beats, heard or remembered, of the vast herds of bison ("American buffalo") that once roamed the American West. The sound recedes as the mother journeys east, but its disappearance also suggests both the decimation of the bison population and the destruction of the Indian way of life that depended on it. Overhunting by both whites and Indians had driven the bison to near extinction by the 1880s; a drought extending from 1845 into the 1860s accelerated the collapse.

How we, too, Prodigal, once rode off, too[3]—
　Waved Seminary Hill a gay good-bye . . .
We found God lavish there in Colorado
　　But passing sly.

The pebbles sang,[4] the firecat slunk away[5]　　　　17
　And glistening through the sluggard freshets came
In golden syllables loosed from the clay
　　His gleaming name.

3. The parable of the Prodigal Son appears in Luke 15:11–22; Crane's capitalization of "Prodigal" makes it clear that the word is a vocative addressed to the son, Larry, rather than an adjective modifying "we, too," although the latter usage persists as an undertone. The Prodigal Son was a young man who left home for a "far country" and squandered his inheritance in riotous living. So famished he craved even pig slops, the Prodigal slunk home, hoping only to be hired as a servant. Instead, he was welcomed by his rejoicing father, who slaughtered the "fatted calf" for a celebratory feast. Crane's Prodigal inverts the parable: he is forgiven in advance by his mother, but his fate remains uncertain at best: he may, or may not, return (but not to home and mother) as the drunken sailor in the next section of *The Bridge*, "Cutty Sark."

4. The singing pebbles are the gleaming nuggets ("syllables") of ore separated from the clay by prospectors panning for gold in the freshets of mountain streams. The images recall William Blake's poem "The Clod and the Pebble":

"Love seeketh not itself to please,
Nor for itself hath any care,
But for another gives its ease,
And builds a heaven in hell's despair."

So sung a little Clod of Clay,
Trodden with the cattle's feet,
But a Pebble of the brook
Warbled out these metres meet:

"Love seeketh only Self to please,
To bind another to its delight,
Joys in another's loss of ease,
And builds a hell in heaven's despite."

For Blake the pebble's song is a necessary corrective to the clod's moralism; for Crane's maternal speaker it is a kind of siren song that spurns the clod's pastoral meekness in favor of the illusion that the gold is a divine gift.

5. Wallace Stevens's poem "Earthy Anecdote" (published in Stevens's *Harmonium* in 1923) introduces the enigmatic firecat, perhaps a distant relative of the Cheshire cat in Lewis Carroll's *Alice's Adventures in Wonderland*. The firecat bristles to ward off noisy, belligerent efforts to claim territory: "Every time the bucks went clattering / Over Oklahoma / A firecat bristled in the way." Stevens's claimed that the bucks were "actual animals," but the poem is essentially a beast fable, so the figurative uses of "buck"—slang for a rowdy young white man, often a cowboy, but also a racially marked epithet for a vigorous, therefore dangerous, young black man or Indian warrior—remain in effect. Oklahoma's Indians, like Colorado's, were displaced and brutalized in the later nineteenth century; some Indian legends involve a cougar or mountain lion that bears fire. Stevens's parable deals primarily with the bristling of poetic imagination against earthy literal-mindedness; in a typical reversal, Crane's firecat slinks away as an even more literal earthiness corrupts the imagination.

A dream called Eldorado was his town,[6]
  It rose up shambling in the nuggets' wake,[7]
It had no charter but a promised crown
    Of claims to stake.

But we,—too late, too early, howsoever—   25
  Won nothing out of fifty-nine—those years—
But gilded promise, yielded to us never,
    And barren tears . . .

The long trail back! I huddled in the shade
  Of wagon-tenting looked out once and saw
Bent westward, passing on a stumbling jade
    A homeless squaw—[8]

6. The myth of "El Dorado," literally "The Golden One," originated in the sixteenth century, when it referred to a mythical South American chieftain who, it was said, ritually covered himself with gold dust before diving into a pure mountain lake. Later the term applied to a lost or distant city of gold and jewels, at first understood by European explorers to be a real place and later treated as a metaphor for any utopia of riches or other transcendental dream. The latter is its sense in the most famous treatment of El Dorado in American literature, Edgar Allen Poe's short poem of the same name. Poe's questing (and singing) knight, like the various wanderers in *The Bridge*, fails to find El Dorado and is finally told to seek it "Over the mountains / Of the Moon, / Down the Valley of the Shadow." But "El Dorado" is not exclusively literary here; it was the original name of the town later known as Colorado City, the present-day Colorado Springs and the epicenter of the Pike's Peak gold rush.

7. In mining terminology, "shambling" is an operation in which ore is thrown successively onto a rising series of platforms ("shambles") and thus brought to a level from which it can be easily retrieved. Crane's metaphor identifies the rapid growth of El Dorado, the Colorado town, with the shambling of gold that helped power it, but the wording is sufficiently ambiguous that "shambling" also retains its more ordinary sense of a clumsy shuffling, suggesting that the lure of this El Dorado, like that of all its dreamlike counterparts, is deceptive.

8. The episode of the homeless squaw is a detailed reworking of section 6 of Whitman's "The Sleepers":

> Now what my mother told me one day as we sat at dinner together,
> Of when she was a nearly grown girl living home with her parents on the old homestead.
>
> A red squaw came one breakfast-time to the old homestead,
> On her back she carried a bundle of rushes for rush-bottoming chairs,
>
> Her hair, straight, shiny, coarse, black, profuse, half-envelop'd her face,
> Her step was free and elastic, and her voice sounded exquisitely as she spoke.
>
> My mother look'd in delight and amazement at the stranger,
> She look'd at the freshness of her tall-borne face and full and pliant limbs,
> The more she look'd upon her she loved her,
> Never before had she seen such wonderful beauty and purity,
> She made her sit on a bench by the jamb of the fireplace, she cook'd food for her,
> She had no work to give her, but she gave her remembrance and fondness.
>
> The red squaw staid all the forenoon, and toward the middle of the afternoon she went
>   away,

Perhaps a halfbreed. On the slender back   33
   She cradled a babe's body, riding without rein.
Her eyes, strange for an Indian's, were not black
     But sharp with pain

And like twin stars.[9] They seemed to shun the gaze
   Of all our silent men—the long team line—
Until she saw me—when the violet haze
     Lit with love shine . . .

I held you up—I suddenly the bolder,   41
   Knew that mere words could not have brought us nearer.
She nodded—and that smile across her shoulder
     Will still endear her[10]

As long as Jim, your father's memory, is warm.
   Yes, Larry, now you're going to sea, remember
You were the first—before Ned and this farm,—
     First-born, remember—

And since then—all that's left to me of Jim   49
   Whose folks, like mine, came out of Arrowhead.
And you're the only one with eyes like him—
     Kentucky bred!

> O my mother was loth to have her go away,
> All the week she thought of her, she watch'd for her many a month,
> She remember'd her many a winter and many a summer,
> But the red squaw never came nor was heard of there again.

Crane replaces the bundle of rushes with a baby to create the moment of communion, which "implies," as Crane observed in a letter to Otto Kahn (September 12, 1927), the pioneer mother's "accession to the nature-symbolism of Pocahontas" relinquished by the squaw. But the meeting is a moment of surrender for both women: the displaced squaw, traveling west, carries her son away from his true home, while the displaced pioneer woman, traveling east, returns to the home (in Indiana, formerly Indian territory) that her son is about to abandon. Each destiny is tragic in its own way.

9. The twin stars are probably the Morning and Evening stars; the two are actually the same celestial body, the planet Venus. The twinning of the stars parallels the twinning of the poem's two women, one as her people's sun is setting, the other as her people's sun is rising.

10. Charges of sentimentality in stanzas 8–11 led Crane to defend them in a letter to William Wright (November 21, 1930): "Since 'race' is the principal motivation of 'Indiana,' I can't help thinking that, observed in the proper perspective, and judged in relation to the argument or theme of the Pocahontas section as a whole, the pioneer woman's maternalism isn't excessive."

I'm standing still, I'm old, I'm half of stone![11]

  Oh, hold me in those eyes' engaging blue;

There's where the stubborn years gleam and atone,—

    Where gold is true!

Down the dim turnpike to the river's edge—   57

  Perhaps I'll hear the mare's hoofs to the ford . . .

Write me from Rio . . . and you'll keep your pledge;

    I know your word!

Come back to Indiana—not too late!

  (Or will you be a ranger to the end?)

Good-by . . . Good-bye . . . oh, I shall always wait

    You Larry, traveller—

        stranger,

           son,

             —my friend—

---

11. The mother "half of stone" recalls the classical figure of Niobe, Queen of Thebes. Niobe boasted that, being the mother of fourteen children, she was superior to the goddess Leto, who had only two. Leto, offended, promptly ordered the two, Apollo and Artemis, to kill all of Niobe's fourteen—seven apiece, the sons and daughters, respectively. Overwhelmed with grief, Niobe fled to Mt. Siplyon in Asia Minor, where she turned to stone and formed a stream from the tears that her petrified form continued to shed in unending mourning. The "barren tears" of the seventh stanza anticipate the mother's metapmorphosis into a half-Niobe, or, with reference to the last stanza's "I will always wait," into a maternal Penelope, who incarnates home as an El Dorado to be sought but never quite found.

4. South Street Seaport, 1901.

III. CUTTY SARK

O, the navies old and oaken
O, the Temeraire no more!

—Melville

CUTTY SARK: This poem concludes the first half of *The Bridge* (Crane to Caresse Crosby, December 26, 1929). The title is the name both of a clipper ship, famous for its role in the nineteenth-century tea trade, and of Crane's favorite whisky, first marketed in 1923. "Cutty Sark" is Scots for "short shift," in other words, a revealing nightgown; in Robert Burns's poem "Tam o' Shanter," the phrase describes the seductive state of undress of a young witch in whose pursuit the drunken hero is almost drowned. Crane picks up the themes of drunkenness and the supernatural but displaces the object of desire from the female siren to the always-feminine ships. To Otto Kahn (September 12, 1927), Crane wrote that "'Cutty Sark' is built on the plan of a *fugue*. Two 'voices'—that of the world of Time, and that of the world of Eternity—are interwoven in the action. The Atlantis theme (that of Eternity) is the transmuted voice of the nickel-slot pianola, and this voice alternates with that of the derelict sailor and the description of the action. The airy regatta of phantom clipper ships seen from Brooklyn Bridge on the way home is quite effective, I think. It was a pleasure to use historical names for these lovely ghosts. Music still haunts their names long after the wind has left their sails."

EPIGRAPH: The concluding lines of "Temeraire," a poem from Herman Melville's *Battle-Pieces* (1866). The *Temeraire* was a British ship of the line, known as "The Fighting *Temeraire*" after it played a key role in Lord Horatio Nelson's victory over Napoleon's fleet at the Battle of Trafalgar in 1805. Decommissioned in 1838, it was towed to land by a tug to be broken up; Melville takes this event, which also inspired a famous painting by J. M. W. Turner, to epitomize the replacement of oaken ships by ironclads and skilled seamanship by modern technology. The concluding section of "Temeraire" reads:

> But Trafalgar is over now,
>   The quarter-deck undone;
> The carved and castled navies fire
>   Their evening-gun.
> O, Tital Temeraire,
>   Your stern-lights fade away;
> Your bulwarks to the years must yield,
>   And heart-of-oak decay.
> A pigmy steam-tug tows you,
>   Gigantic, to the shore—
> Dismantled of your guns and spars,
>   And sweeping wings of war.
> The rivets clinch the iron-clads,
>   Men learn a deadlier lore;
> But Fame has nailed your battle-flags—
>   Your ghost it sails before:
> O, the navies old and oaken,
>   O, the Temeraire no more!

I met a man in South Street,[1] tall—
a nervous shark tooth swung on his chain.
His eyes pressed through green glass
—green glasses, or bar lights made them
so—

    shine—

       GREEN—

           eyes—[2]   5

stepped out—forgot to look at you
or left you several blocks away—

in the nickel-in-the-slot piano jogged
"Stamboul[3] Nights"—weaving somebody's nickel[4]—sang—

1. South Street Seaport, in lower Manhattan, became the most important commercial maritime center in the United States after the opening of the Erie Canal in 1826. The figure of the drunken sailor is a composite of the homeward-bound Columbus of "Ave Maria," the prodigal son Larry, who goes to sea in "Indiana," and two famous literary seafarers, the Ishmael of Melville's *Moby-Dick* and the title character of Samuel Taylor Coleridge's *Rime of the Ancient Mariner*.

2. The old sailor resembles Coleridge's Ancient Mariner in both his compulsive talking and his "glittering eyes"; the eyes hold the listener captive: "He holds him with his glittering eye—/ The Wedding Guest stood still,/ And listened like a three-year's child:/ The Mariner hath his will" (ll. 13–16). The green of the sailor's eyes reflects—literally—the green glass of the whiskey bottles and the green lights of the bar, but the phrase " GREEN—eyes" may also suggest a pun on "green ice": when the Ancient Mariner's ship enters the south polar seas, it encounters "ice,/ Mast high . . ./ As green as emerald." "Mist and snow" are present, too, connecting this Antarctic voyage to the "white Arctic" of "Cutty Sark," discussed below.

3. "Stamboul," a contraction for "Istanbul," marks the limit of western Asia, as Japan will subsequently mark the limit of East Asia; touching both points, the ships evoked in "Cutty Sark" trace a circle around the globe. Istanbul's location on a strait, the Bosporus, associates it with two other straits with symbolic value for the poem: the Dardanelles and the Strait of Gibraltar. The fabled lost city of Atlantis, a utopia mythologically recovered by *The Bridge* in "Atlantis," its concluding section, supposedly lay just west of Gibraltar, through whose strait the Atlantic meets the western Mediterranean. The Dardanelles, at the eastern end of the Mediterranean just south of the Bosporus, is the site of the legend of the Greek Leander, who swam the strait nightly to reach his lover, Hero, until he was drowned in the crossing; the legend arises toward the end of "Cutty Sark" when the clipper ship *Leander* is named, and again in the epigraph to "Three Songs." *Stamboul Nights* was the name of a book on Turkey published in 1921 by H. D. Dwight, a former American consular official; Crane seems to have borrowed the title so that the song, aside from suggesting exotic romance, could combine suggestions of utopian longing and nocturnal romance.

4. The nickel is the same as the one that appears in "Van Winkle" and will appear again in "The Tunnel." Given the preoccupation of *The Bridge* with the history of the American Indians, it may also be significant that in Crane's day the nickel would have been the so-called Indian Head. This coin (minted between 1913 and 1938) had a buffalo etched on the reverse with the head of an Indian on the obverse. Crane's sailor, like Maquokeeta in "The Dance," wears an ornamental tooth.

Murmurs of Leviathan he spoke,[5]
and rum was Plato in our heads[6] . . .

"It's *S.S. Ala*[7]—Antwerp—now remember kid
to put me out at three she sails on time.
I'm not much good at time any more keep   15
weakeyed watches sometimes snooze—"[8] his bony hands
got to beating time . . . "A whaler once—
I ought to keep time and get over it—I'm a
Democrat—I know what time it is—No
I don't want to know what time it is[9]—that   20

5. The "Murmurs of Leviathan" is the first of a series of allusions merging Crane's old sailor and the Ancient Mariner with the figure of Melville's Ishmael—Ishmael repeatedly identifies Moby Dick with the biblical Leviathan—while also setting up resonances with the suffering of Job (Job 41) and God's redemptive promise to Isaiah to kill Leviathan (Isaiah 27). Like the Ancient Mariner, Ishmael returns, the sole survivor of a catastrophic sea voyage, with a compulsion to tell everything that happened.

6. . The association of rum, that is, of drunkenness, with Plato recalls the argument of Plato's Dialogue *Ion*, which argues that poets are inspired by a divine rapture, akin to madness, and do not understand what they say. Crane's text develops several of Plato's leading images: the wing, the effect of music, and an intoxicating drink—though rum, the sailor's portion, is an obviously debased version of Plato's "milk and honey": the poets "are not in their right minds when they make their beautiful songs, but they are like Corybants with their wits dancing about. As soon as they mount on their harmony and rhythm, they become frantic and possessed; just as the Bacchantic women, possessed and out of their senses, draw milk and honey out of the rivers. . . . For the poet is an airy thing, a winged and a holy thing; and he cannot make poetry until he becomes inspired and goes out of his senses."

7. "*Ala*" is presumably a drunken error for "Antwerp," but an *ala* is also a wing or an anatomical part in winglike form. This slip of the tongue thus connects the movement of the clipper ships and their winglike sails with the flight of Plato's poetic inspiration. The allusion will resurface later in the name of one of the ships, *Ariel*.

8. Another allusion to Melville's Ishmael, echoed in the next line by "'A whaler once . . .'" In chapter 35 of *Moby-Dick*, "The Mast -Head," Ishmael recounts how he often kept "but sorry guard" during the watches, being "lulled into . . . an opium-like listlessness of vacant reverie . . . by the blending cadence of waves with thoughts."

9. The repetition of "know what time" is reminiscent of the similar repetition of " HURRY UP PLEASE IT'S TIME," also set in a dive (a seedy British pub at closing) in "A Game of Chess," the second section of Eliot's *The Waste Land*.

damned white Arctic killed my time . . ."[10]

O Stamboul Rose—drums weave—

"I ran a donkey engine down there on the Canal
in Panama—got tired of that—
then Yucatan selling kitchenware—beads—   25
have you seen Popocatepetl[11]—birdless mouth
with ashes sifting down—?
                              and then the coast again . . ."

Rose of Stamboul O coral Queen
Teased remnants of the skeletons of cities—
and galleries, galleries of watergutted lava   30
snarling stone—green—drums—drown—[12]

10. In Chapter 42 of *Moby-Dick,* "The Whiteness of the Whale," Melville describes a consuming terror identified with whiteness: when we "consider that the mystical cosmetic which produces every one of [Nature's] hues, the great principle of light, forever remains white or colorless in itself, and if operating without medium upon matter, would touch all objects, even tulips and roses, with its own blank tinge—pondering all this, the palsied universe lies before us a leper." Like the Ancient Mariner, Ishmael voyages into an abyss of meaninglessness from which he never quite emerges, and so does Crane's old sailor. The shift of whiteness from the great whale to the damned Arctic suggests the ill-fated polar expeditions of the early twentieth century, together with their fictional Antarctic forerunner, Edgar Allen Poe's "The Narrative of A. Gordon Pym," which ends with an inexplicable vision of white terror: "Many gigantic and pallidly white birds flew continuously now from beyond the veil. . . . And now we rushed into the embraces of the cataract, where a chasm threw itself open to receive us. But there arose in our pathway a shrouded human figure, very far larger in its proportions than any dweller among men. And the hue of the skin of the figure was of the perfect whiteness of the snow."

11. In Mesoamerican mythology, the self-immolating god Quetzalcoatl (see "The Dance") traveled to the sea over two mountains. One, Popocatépetl, was a volcano, whose crater forms the text's "birdless mouth" with dropping ashes, an image of nullified inspiration (a speechless mouth, a space without wing or birdsong; compare Eliot's "Dead mountain mouth of carious teeth that cannot spit" from "What the Thunder Said," the fifth section of *The Waste Land.*) The other mountain was Ixaccíhuatl, the White Woman, corresponding to the "glacier woman" mentioned in l. 2 of "The Dance," but here displaced into the submerged "coral Queen" of l. 29.

12. "Rose of Stamboul" tacitly introduces the theme of Atlantis, whose sunken form is invoked by the sound of the song. The lost heritage of the Americas is like the great lost city that, according to legend, long ago sank to the sea floor, where its buildings are worn away to skeletal forms and the cultural treasures of its galleries "drown." (The image of the rose is actually migrating westward, as we will see shortly.)

Sing!

"—that spiracle!"[13] he shot a finger out the door . . .

"O life's a geyser—beautiful—my lungs—

No—I can't live on land—"[14]   35

I saw the frontiers gleaming of his mind;

or are there frontiers—running sands sometimes

running sands—somewhere—sands running . . .

Or they may start some white machine that sings.[15]

Then you may laugh and dance the axletree—[16]   40

steel—silver—kick the traces—and know—

     ATLANTIS ROSE[17] *drums wreathe the rose,*

     the star floats burning in a gulf of tears[18]

     and sleep another thousand—

13. The spiracle, the whale's breathing spout, is the subject of two chapters, 51 and 85, of *Moby-Dick*; the former seems particularly pertinent here in view of the immediately following "life's a geyser—beautiful." Chapter 51, "The Spirit-Spout," describes the recurrent appearance by night of the watery jet from a whale's spiracle; the sight is both beautiful and mysterious: "On such a silent night a silvery jet was seen far in advance of the bubbles at the bow. Lit up by the moon, it looked celestial; seemed some plumed and glittering god arising from the sea."

14. In Chapter 1 of *Moby-Dick*, Ishmael says much the same: "Whenever I find myself growing grim about the mouth; whenever it is a damp, drizzly November in my soul; whenever I find myself involuntarily pausing before coffin warehouses . . . —then, I account it high time to get to sea as soon as I can."

15. The pianola that has been playing in the background. But the image anticipates the representation of the Bridge in "Atlantis."

16. The axletree is a fixed axle with terminal spindles on which carriage wheels revolve; the wheels' circular motion corresponds to the circling of the globe by sailing ships, the poem's model for all voyages of discovery. With the ambivalence typical of "Cutty Sark," dancing the axletree may suggest both drunken reeling and the traditional circular dance of the cosmos.

17. "Stamboul Rose" now becomes "Atlantis Rose," and the phrase is a pun. It may state that the sunken city of Atlantis rose—has arisen—from the sea, a vision of utopia, or it may designate an object or image, a rose of Atlantis or Atlantis as a rose, perhaps even a compass rose, the ornamental design on a map representing the directions of the eight major winds; the rose is a traditional mystic symbol of perfection and cosmic harmony, invoked at the end of Dante's *Divine Comedy* (in conjunction with "The love that moves the sun and the other stars") as a consummate figure for both. On either reading, the image of Atlantis is present only in the sound of the music, which, we are about to discover, has long since stopped. Like much else in "Cutty Sark," the mysterious "Atlantis Rose" points to both an ideal and the degradation of the ideal.

18. According to the ancient myth, when the weeping god Quetzalcoatl immolated himself by the sea, he became the Morning Star, a transformation already invoked early in "The Dance" and reprised there when the chieftain Maquokeeta is burned at the stake.

interminably

long since somebody's nickel—stopped—   45

playing—

A wind worried those wicker-neat lapels, the

swinging summer entrances to cooler hells . . .

Outside a wharf truck nearly ran him down[19]

—he lunged up Bowery way while the dawn   50

was putting the Statue of Liberty out[20]—that

torch of hers you know—

I started walking home across the Bridge . . .

*   *   *[21]

Blithe Yankee vanities, turreted sprites, winged

British repartees, skil-

ful savage sea-girls[22]   55

that bloomed in the spring—Heave, weave

those bright designs the trade winds drive . . .[23]

---

19. The wharf truck recalls "The Harbor Dawn," where "a truck will lumber past the wharves."

20. The image of the Statue of Liberty at dawn echoes "To Brooklyn Bridge," which opens with the same idea. *The Bridge* at this point seems to have arrived at its own beginning, an impression reinforced by the emblematic value of the next line, which names the Bridge and identifies it as the way home—home, as it were, to Atlantis.

21. The ellipsis divides "Cutty Sark" into disjunct, unequal parts; as the broken-down old sailor wanders off, the glamorous world of the clipper ships and their circumnavigation of the globe loom as a vision ("clipper dreams indelible"), perhaps as an extension of "the hallucinations incident to rum-drinking in a South Street dive" (Crane to Otto Kahn, September 12, 1927) or as a poetic (Coleridgean?) opium dream. The role of clipper ships in the opium trade quickly comes up: "*Sweet opium and tea, Yo-ho!*"

22. The sea-girls (like the vanities, sprites, and repartees) are the clipper ships themselves, with their feminine figureheads and traditional designation as "she." The image suggests a positive form of the dangerously seductive "cutty sark" of Burns's "Tam o'Shanter," echoed in the next line in the "bright designs," the flags or ensigns flown by the ships, extended by the "bright skysails" six lines later, and topped off by the "pennants" two lines after that.

23. Heaving and weaving are jobs that sailors may perform on any day at sea. Given the motifs of "Stamboul Nights" and "Stamboul Rose," the most pertinent allusion may be to the sailors' weaving of a Turkshead, a pattern of rope braiding used to make mats and bracelets. The weaving of the ships on the ocean may also be a metaphor for the weaving of the words on the page. When Crane calls the ships "repartees," he suggests their identification with language, an idea echoed by the image of the ships "ticketing the Line," in which the Line, the equator or other great circle of the earth, may carry the overtone of a line of type or poetry.

5. The Bridge and Manhattan Skyline, ca. 1915.

Sweet opium and tea, Yo-ho! [24]
Pennies for porpoises that bank the keel![25]
Fins whip the breeze around Japan!   60

Bright skysails ticketing the Line, wink round the Horn
To Frisco, Melbourne . . .
                    Pennants, parabolas—
clipper dreams indelible and ranging,

24. At this point, the song is no longer the pianola's but a sea chantey running through the poet's head. "Sweet opium and tea" combines the motif of intoxication with the clippers' participation in the China tea trade, for which the *Cutty Sark* was expressly designed. (The opium was no doubt a bonus.)

25. In maritime lore porpoises that play about a ship near land are good omens. According to "Cetology," chapter 32 of *Moby-Dick*, "Their appearance is generally hailed with delight by the mariner. Full of fine spirits, they invariably come from the breezy billows to windward. They are the lads that always live before the wind." Pitching pennies into the water may be a way of wishing for the porpoises, linked in the poem to putting "somebody's nickel" into the slot of the pianola.

baronial white on lucky blue!

    Perennial-*Cutty*-trophied-*Sark!*[26]   65

Thermopylae, Black Prince, Flying Cloud through Sunda[27]
—scarfed of foam, their bellies veered green esplanades,
locked in wind-humors, ran their eastings down;[28]

    at Java Head freshened the nip
    (sweet opium and tea!)   70
    and turned and left us on the lee . . .

Buntlines tusseling (91 days, 20 hours and anchored!)
        Rainbow,[29] *Leander*[30]
(last trip a tragedy)—where can you be
Nimbus?[31] and you rivals two—

26. "Trophied" because the clipper ships raced each other from China to London; the ship that arrived with the first tea of the year stood to make large profits.

27. The ships named from here to the end are all real and increasingly bear symbolic names. Crane wrote to Malcolm and Peggy Cowley: "It happens that all the clippers mentioned were real beings [and] had extensive histories in the Tea trade—and the last two mentioned were life-long rivals. Rather touching" ((July 29, 1926); in a later letter he refers "this airy regatta of phantom clipper ships seen from Brooklyn Bridge" (to Otto Kahn, September 12, 1927). The *Thermopylae* raced the *Cutty Sark* from Shanghai to London in 1872. The *Cutty Sark* initially took a four-hundred-mile lead, but it hit a storm near the Cape of Good Hope and lost its rudder in the Sunda Strait. The captain built a makeshift replacement. The *Thermopylae* reached London a week before the *Cutty Sark*, but the latter became renowned for sailing so far with an improvised rudder. The *Thermopylae* and the *Cutty Sark* raced often in the 1880s, with the *Cutty Sark* winning regularly, often breaking speed records.

28. Lines 67–68 describe the turning of the clipper ships onto an easterly course toward home. Laden with the "sweet opium and tea" of l. 70 as if with the riches of Cathay, the ships turn as the wind veers, that is, shifts in a clockwise direction; the turn is so smooth and swift that the sea lane acts as an esplanade for the vessels' gliding. The movement suggests the freedom and romance of Crane's "airy regatta," but the green of the esplanades recalls the green glasses of the waterfront dive and the ships, "locked in wind-humors," remain subject to chance and misfortune.

29. The *Rainbow* made four trips to China but was lost on its fourth voyage.

30. The *Leander* made several voyages to China before being sold repeatedly; it was broken up by its Persian owner in 1901. As noted earlier, Leander, a figure from Greek myth, was in love with the priestess Hero, who lived on the opposite shore of the Hellespont (the Dardanelles). Guided by a light in her tower, he would swim to her every night; on a night when the light was extinguished, Leander drowned ("last trip a tragedy").

31. A nimbus is both natural (a rain cloud) and supernatural (a halo).

A long tack keeping—

       Taeping?

       Ariel?[32]

32. The *Taeping* and the *Ariel* were two of the most famous clipper ships in the China tea trade. They once engaged in a six-thousand-mile race, which both ships completed in ninety days. The *Taeping* won by twenty minutes, but the *Ariel* had her cargo completely unloaded first. By concluding with the name *Ariel*, Crane makes a culminating allusion to the famous sprite of Shakespeare's *The Tempest*, who, among other things, controls the destiny of passing ships and is responsible for the mysterious music that permeates the island on which the play is set. The lines of Ariel's best-known song suggest an ideal synopsis of "Cutty Sark" and perhaps a phantom template for it:

Full fathom five thy father lies;
Of his bones are coral made;
These are pearls that were his eyes;
Nothing of him that doth fade
But doth suffer a sea-change
Into something rich and strange.
Sea-nymphs hourly ring his knell.

Compare Crane's "*O coral Queen—/ teased remnants of the skeletons of cities.*" Eliot quotes "These are pearls that were his eyes" in section 2 of *The Waste Land*, "A Game of Chess"; Crane may allude to both sources at the beginning of "Cutty Sark" when he describes the drunken sailor's eyes as "pressed against green glass" and subsequently as transformed into " GREEN—/ eyes." The sailor later refers to his keeping "weakeyed watches" (l. 15), which leads the narrator to remark on his "bony hands . . . beating time." Beating time connects to the motif of music ("*O Stamboul Rose*"), subsequently linked to the lost city of Atlantis, and thus perhaps to the knell rung by the sea nymphs—the phantom clipper ships.

IV. CAPE HATTERAS

The seas all crossed,
weathered the capes, the voyage done . . .

—*Walt Whitman*

CAPE HATTERAS: A cape on the North Carolina coast, notorious both for its treacherous ocean currents and its frequent destructive hurricanes. Hatteras includes the towns of Kill Devil Hills, where Orville Wright piloted the flight of the first airplane, invented with his brother Wilbur, on December 17, 1903, and nearby Kitty Hawk, commonly mistaken for the location of the flight.

EPIGRAPH: From Whitman's "Passage to India," l. 220. Whitman's 1872 poem takes the achievements of nineteenth-century technology bridging eastern and western locales—the opening of the Suez Canal, the laying of the Atlantic cable, the completion of the transcontinental railroad—as the completion of the work of discovery begun by Columbus's sea voyages and as a metaphor for spiritual accomplishment. "Cape Hatteras" extends both the completion and the metaphor through the twentieth-century technology of flight.

Imponderable the dinosaur
>> sinks slow,
>>> the mammoth saurian
>>>> ghoul,[1] the eastern
>>>>> Cape . . .[2]
While rises in the west the coastwise range,[3]
>>> slowly the hushed land—
Combustion at the astral core—the dorsal change
Of energy—convulsive shift of sand . . .[4]
But we, who round the cape, the promontories   5
Where strange tongues vary messages of surf
Below grey citadels, repeating to the stars
The ancient names—return home to our own
Hearths, there to eat an apple and recall
The songs that gypsies dealt us at Marseille[5]   10
Or how the priests walked—slowly through Bombay—[6]
Or to read you, Walt,—knowing us in thrall

1. The site of frequent shipwrecks, Cape Hatteras was (and is) known as "The Graveyard of the Atlantic." The epithet helps explain the predatory image of the "saurian ghoul" and the subsequent use of "ghoul mound" (ll. 178, 224), suggesting a fresh grave, to describe the slope of the land.

2. "The eastern Cape" may be meant to establish Hatteras as a geographical complement to Cape Horn, the southernmost point of South America; the dividing line between the Atlantic and the Pacific lies along the meridian of the southern cape. Like Cape Hatteras, Cape Horn is especially treacherous, but until the opening of the Panama Canal in 1914 rounding it—"weathering" it, to recall Whitman's term from the epigraph—was an essential part of the clipper-ship voyages evoked by Crane in "Cutty Sark."

3. The Blue Ridge and Appalachian mountains of western North Carolina.

4. The images of combustion, change of energy, and shift of sand refer obliquely to the Wright Brothers' flight (the firing engine, the turning propellers, and the shifting sand in the dunes of Kill Devil Hills); the combustion is "astral" because the stars, whose "ancient names" (l. 8) provided guides to navigation at sea, now appear to burn with a primordial energy tapped to power the aircraft.

5. Crane greatly enjoyed a stay in Marseilles during May and June 1929; he completed "Cape Hatteras" in September. The connection of the memory to eating an apple is probably a coy sexual allusion; a letter from Marseilles (to Harry Crosby, May 16, 1929) reports: "Had a great time last Saturday visiting the whore houses with an English sailor—whose great expression of assent and agreement was 'heave Ho!' " The gypsy songs continue the motif of the poet as itinerant quester on the model of Whitman, who presides over "Cape Hatteras" and whom Crane is about to apostrophize for the first time.

6. The reference to Bombay (present day Mumbai) continues the link with Whitman's "Passage to India" started by the epigraph. Whitman does not refer to Bombay specifically, but he does treat India as an ancient source of "the far-darting beams of the spirit, the unloos'd dreams," the "elder religions" and "fables spurning the known," all of which he recapitulates ("resumes") on American soil: "The old, most populous, wealthiest of earth's lands, / The streams of the Indus and the Ganges and their many affluents, / (I my shores of America walking to-day behold, resuming all)" (ll. 128–30).

To that deep wonderment, our native clay   71

Whose depth of red, eternal flesh of Pocahontas—[7]

Those continental folded aeons, surcharged   15

With sweetness below derricks, chimneys, tunnels—[8]

Is veined by all that time has really pledged us . . .[9]

And from above, thin squeaks of radio static,

The captured fume of space foam in our ears—

What whisperings of far watches on the main   20

Relapsing into silence,[10] while time clears

Our lenses, lifts a focus, resurrects

A periscope to glimpse what joys or pain

Our eyes could share or answer—then deflects

Us, shunting to a labyrinth[11] submersed   25

Where each sees only his dim past reversed. . . .

But that star-glistered salver of infinity,

The circle, blind crucible of endless space,

7. "Cape Hatteras" takes Whitman as representative of the spiritual body of America, a masculine counterpart to Pocahontas and, like her, perennially present in the "deep wonderment" of "our native clay." In the famous concluding passage of "Song of Myself," Whitman enjoins the reader, "If you want me again look for me under your boot soles." Whitman often makes intimate addresses to his posterity: "It avails not, time nor place—distance avails not, / I am with you, men and women of a generation, or ever so many generations hence" ("Crossing Brooklyn Ferry," ll. 20–21). By casting himself as the companion and lover of Whitman, Crane in "Cape Hatteras" fulfills the elder poet's prophecy, or at least "resumes" its promise despite the destructive energies that come with modernity.

8. The "folded aeons" are rock strata "surcharged," that is, both overlaid and enriched, with the "sweetness" of the fertile "native clay." Clay is traditionally the earthy substance transmuted into flesh, here the "red, eternal flesh of Pocahontas." Adam (referred to a few lines below and already intimated by that erotic apple) is often said to have been created from red clay, the word for which in Hebrew may be transliterated as *Adama*.

9. "All that time has really pledged us" recalls the apostrophe in "To Brooklyn Bridge," "Terrific threshold of the prophet's pledge," suggesting a parallel between the veining of the continental body, literally by deposits of ore, and the bridging of eastern and western shores. The veins also suggest the thread left by Ariadne to lead Theseus out of the Cretan Labyrinth, referred to a few lines below.

10. Radio static replaces "whisperings of far watches on the main," as aviation replaces voyaging by sail as the primary means of discovering new worlds; modern experience condenses space into a substance ("captured fume of space foam") and time into an optic for seeing beyond the present (the "resurrected" periscope). But both transitions are troubled; space becomes the distance into which the whisperings relapse into silence, and time, as the next lines indicate, deflects us into a labyrinth that reverses all inherited pledges into dim dead ends.

11. In classical mythology the artificer who constructed the Cretan labyrinth was Daedalus. Confined to a tower to prevent him from revealing the labyrinth's secret, Daedalus (according to Ovid's *Metamorphoses*) fashioned waxen wings on which he and his son Icarus flew away— but Icarus flew too close to the sun, which melted his wings and left him to fall to his death in the sea.

Is sluiced by motion,—subjugated never.[12]
Adam and Adam's answer in the forest   30
Left Hesperus mirrored in the lucid pool.[13]
Now the eagle dominates our days, is jurist
Of the ambiguous cloud. We know the strident rule
Of wings imperious . . . Space, instantaneous,
Flickers a moment, consumes us in its smile: 35
A flash over the horizon—shifting gears
And we have laughter, or more sudden tears.
Dream cancels dream in this new realm of fact
From which we wake into the dream of act;
Seeing himself an atom in a shroud—   40
Man hears himself an engine in a cloud![14]

12. The circle is the "salver of infinity" because its shape, imagined as traced around the concentric spheres of Ptolemaic astronomy, is a traditional symbol of cosmic perfection; the circle is "star-glistered" because the fixed stars were thought to be distributed around the interior of the outermost sphere of the classical cosmos. The metaphor of the crucible suggests both alchemy and the modern chemistry that "resumes" it in Whitman's sense of transformative repetition; the associated metaphor of the salver and its sluicing motion may (picking up on the alchemists' primary goal) suggest the pan of the gold-rush miners who figure in "Indiana." Finally, the circle as applied to the globe is "subjugated never" because sailing ships circumnavigating the earth could not avoid the terrors of the capes. Circumnavigation by airplane was almost as fraught: of the four planes that began the first successful aerial circumnavigation in 1924, one crashed and another capsized after being forced down at sea.

13. In Genesis 2:11, Adam answers God's question "Where art thou?" from among the trees of the Garden of Eden, where he and Eve have hidden themselves after their fall. But Crane is probably conflating two passages from Milton's *Paradise Lost*: one from book 8, where Adam, tested by God, talks back to his creator in a successful attempt to secure a mate (ll. 411–35), and the other from book 4, where Eve is fascinated by her own image in a "clear / Smooth Lake that seemed . . . another sky" (ll. 458–59) until Adam, meeting her for the first time, turns her gaze to him (ll. 460–69). Milton transfers the mirroring to the couple; Eve, God tells Adam, is "Thy likeness, thy fit help, thy other self, / Thy wish, exactly to thy heart's desire" (8:450–51). Crane abstracts the relationship to the mirroring of Hesperus, the Evening Star, in the "lucid"—that is, illuminated, light-reflecting—"pool." The Evening Star is actually the planet Venus and hence an emblem of the heart's desire; it is also, with similar connotations, a reminder of the transformed Quetzalcoatl alluded to in "The Dance" and the Morning Star (also Venus) that closes "The Harbor Dawn." In the unspoiled nature of the Garden of Eden, the Hesperian reflection, descending from heaven to earth, satisfies the desire that it evokes. But the intervention of modernity breaks the mirror of desire. Latter-day desire both literally and figuratively takes to the skies; its ascending medium is unbounded space and its Zarathustran animal is the eagle of the next line, traditionally capable of staring unblinded into the sun—an invulnerable Icarus.

14. Modernity, symbolized by aviation, reverses the traditional conception of "man"; what was formerly seen as a soul housed in a body (an atom in a shroud) is now heard as a body enveloped by the mirage of a soul (an engine in a cloud). The latter image plays ironically on numerous biblical passages in which the voice of God emanates from a cloud.

"—Recorders ages hence"—[15]ah, syllables of faith![16]
Walt, tell me, Walt Whitman, if infinity
Be still the same as when you walked the beach
Near Paumanok[17]—your lone patrol—and heard the wraith   45
Through surf, its bird note there a long time falling . . .
For you, the panoramas and this breed of towers,[18]
Of you—the theme that's statured in the cliff,
O Saunterer on free ways still ahead![19]
Not this our empire yet, but labyrinth   50
Wherein your eyes, like the Great Navigator's[20] without ship,
Gleam from the great stones of each prison crypt
Of canyoned traffic . . .[21] Confronting the Exchange,
Surviving in a world of stocks—they also range
Across the hills where second timber strays   55
Back over Connecticut farms, abandoned pastures—
Sea eyes and tidal, undenying, bright with myth!

15. "Recorders ages hence" refers to a poem in the "Calamus" section of Whitman's
Leaves of Grass in which the poet asks to be remembered above all for wandering hand in
hand with his male lover, "they twain apart from other men"—a wish that "Cape Hatteras"
will conclude by granting, with Crane extending his hand in the lover's role.

16. Crane to Waldo Frank (June 20, 1926): "If only America were half as worthy today to
be spoken of as Whitman spoke of it fifty years ago there might be something for me to say
. . . time has shown how increasingly lonely and ineffectual his confidence stands."

17. Paumanok: the Indian name for Long Island, Whitman's birthplace. The word means
"fish-shaped"; Whitman used it often, notably in "Out of the Cradle Endlessly Rocking," to
which this line and the next allude. The poem recalls an experience in boyhood of walking
along the shore and hearing the mournful cry of a solitary bird bereft of its mate. Sympathy
with the bird's cry gives the boy his vocation as a poet.

18. The breed of towers includes the "derricks and chimneys" referred to earlier (echoing
the "cloud-flown derricks" of "To Brooklyn Bridge") and perhaps recalls the Manhattan
skyline from the conclusion of "The Harbor Dawn" while anticipating the depiction of the
Woolworth Building in a later section, "Virginia." "Passage to India" celebrates "Towers of
fables immortal fashion'd from mortal dreams!" (l. 27).

19. The romance of space requires the lover-poet to assume a new identity as a wanderer,
taking as a model the Whitman who celebrated the "free ways" of the open road: "Afoot and
light-hearted I take to the open road, / Healthy, free, the world before me, / The long brown
path before me leading me wherever I choose" ("Song of the Open Road," ll. 1–3).

20. Columbus.

21. Crane at this point momentarily switches locale. Following Whitman's imagined gaze,
he turns from Cape Hatteras back to New York, with references to the city's "canyoned
traffic" (that is, foot traffic between tall stone buildings) and the Stock Exchange; both references recall images from "To Brooklyn Bridge." From there the gaze passes across the "abandoned pastures" and second-growth forests of Connecticut and finally comes to rest on a
power plant during the night shift. Whitman's eyes become the means of seeing beyond the
deformations of modern life and thus of remaining oriented by the "tidal" pull of discovery
toward an open future still "bright with myth."

The nasal whine of power whips a new universe . . .
Where spouting pillars spoor the evening sky,[22]
Under the looming stacks of the gigantic power house   60
Stars prick the eyes with sharp ammoniac proverbs,[23]
New verities, new inklings in the velvet hummed
Of dynamos where hearing's leash is strummed . . .[24]
Power's script,—wound, bobbin-bound, refined—
Is stropped to the slap of belts on booming spools, spurred   65
Into the bulging bouillon, harnessed jelly of the stars.[25]
Towards what? The forked crash of split thunder parts
Our hearing momentwise;[26] but fast in whirling armatures,
As bright as frogs' eyes, giggling in the girth
Of steely gizzards—axle-bound, confined   70
In coiled precision, bunched in mutual glee
The bearings glint,—O murmurless and shined
In oilrinsed circles of blind ecstasy!

Stars scribble on our eyes the frosty sagas,
The gleaming cantos of unvanquished space . . .[27]   75

22. Spouting pillars: smokestacks, with an ironic play on both the pillar as a symbol of civilization and the biblical image of the pillar of fire by day and pillar of cloud by night by which God led the Israelites on their Exodus out of Egypt (Exodus 13:21–22).

23. The acrid smoke stings eyes that turn their gaze upward to the stars. If the gaze is still Whitman's, its ability to find affirmative truths in the night sky (the poetic equivalent of the skill of the Great Navigator) is countered by the prick of discomfiting proverbs. A passage in Whitman's "On the Beach at Night" suggests the type of vision threatened with obscurity: "The ravening clouds shall not long be victorious, / They shall not long possess the sky, they devour the stars only in apparition, / Jupiter shall emerge, be patient, watch again another night, the Pleiades shall emerge, / They are immortal." (ll. 17–20). Crane alludes to the Pleiades later in "Cape Hatteras."

24. "Hearing's leash": a debased form of the poet's lyre or harp as "resumed" in the cabling of the Bridge. The strings are crudely strummed rather than plucked by artful fingers; the noise of the dynamos is the auditory equivalent of the shrouded stars' ammoniac proverbs.

25. The imagery of winding and spooling suggests a mechanized version of the weaving of the classical Fates, coupled with the familiar metaphor of fate as something written, a sentence in both senses of the term. "Power's script" is whetted ("stropped") and imprinted "to the slap" of the belts driving the dynamos, as if the electrical generators, with their spooling ribbons, were monstrous typewriters. The industrial writing machine reduces the destiny traditionally written in the stars to their "harnessed jelly," raw energy without purpose or meaning ("Towards what?").

26. The peal of thunder may recall the conclusion of Eliot's *The Waste Land*, where what the thunder "says" admonishes those who hear it to question themselves; the thunder is both accusatory and potentially redemptive. Any such effect here is only momentary, as the sound (it never rises to speech) of the thunder is drowned out by the "blind ecstasy" of oiled bearings in mechanical rotation, a travesty of the circle of infinity invoked earlier.

27. At this point, the poem shifts back to Cape Hatteras; the stars cease pricking the eyes (now Crane's rather than Whitman's) and begin, with the text itself, to write the epic of "unvanquished space": the ambivalent history of aviation as aspiration.

O sinewy silver biplane, nudging the wind's withers! [28]
There, from Kill Devils Hill at Kitty Hawk[29]
Two brothers in their twinship left the dune;[30]
Warping the gale,[31] the Wright windwrestlers veered[32]
Capeward, then blading the wind's flank, banked and spun[33]   80
What ciphers risen from prophetic script,
What marathons new-set between the stars![34]
The soul, by naphtha fledged into new reaches
Already knows the closer clasp of Mars,—
New latitudes, unknotting, soon give place   85
To what fierce schedules, rife of doom apace!

Behold the dragons' covey—amphibian, ubiquitous
To hedge the seaboard, wrap the headland, ride
The blue's cloud-templed districts unto ether . . .[35]

28. "The wind's withers": the plane mounts the wind as a man does a horse, fusing mechanical with bodily energy. The equestrian image is heroic, modulating later into martial prowess, then into rampant destructiveness.

29. The correct name is Kill Devil Hills; the site is four miles from Kitty Hawk, from which the Wrights telegraphed the news of their successful flight.

30. "Twinship": The Wrights' Flyer was a biplane. But only one brother, Orville, left the dune in it for the twelve-second flight.

31. The flight "warps" the gale by turning into a headwind toward the Cape. The term applies to sailing as well as to aviation, continuing the relationship between Columbus's ships and the Wrights' airship.

32. This line and the next recall Gerard Manley Hopkins's "The Windhover":

I caught this morning morning's minion, king-
dom of daylight's dauphin, dapple-dawn-drawn Falcon, in his riding
Of the rolling level underneath him steady air, and striding
High there, how he run upon the rein of a wimpling wing
In his ecstasy! then off, off forth on swing,
As a skate's heel sweeps smooth on a bow-bend: the hurl and gliding
Rebuffed the big wind. (ll.1–7)

33. This line and the previous one transmute the imagery of weaving associated with the power plant: "warping," the lengthwise arrangement of yarn on a loom, "blading," the turning of a yarn spindle, and spinning again produce a form of writing, the "ciphers risen from prophetic script" of the next line. But this is also a kind of skywriting; each of the terms cited literally applies to the operation or motion of the plane.

34. Marathons: uncapitalized, the word refers less to the famous battle between the Athenians and Persians in 490 BCE than to the long-distance race that derives its name from the battle. Efforts at long-distance flight largely defined the heroic questing of early aviation, most famously in Charles Lindbergh's solo transatlantic flight of 1927. But the turn, after this line, to the use of planes as weapons of war does seem to develop the military subtext of "marathon."

35. The "cloud-templed districts" recall Prospero's rueful lines from Shakespeare's The Tempest: "The cloud-capp'd tow'rs, the gorgeous palaces, / The solemn temples, the great globe itself, / Yea, all which it inherit, shall dissolve, / And . . . leave not a rack behind" (4.1.152–56).

While Iliads glimmer through eyes raised in pride 90
Hell's belt springs wider into heaven's plumed side.³⁶
O bright circumferences, heights employed to fly
War's fiery kennel³⁷ masked in downy offings,—
This tournament of space, the threshed and chiseled height,
Is baited by marauding circles, bludgeon flail 95
Of rancorous grenades whose screaming petals carve us
Wounds that we wrap with theorems sharp as hail!³⁸

Wheeled swiftly, wings emerge from larval-silver hangars.
Taut motors surge, space-gnawing, into flight;
Through sparkling visibility, outspread, unsleeping, 100
Wings clip the last peripheries of light . . .
Tellurian wind-sleuths on dawn patrol,³⁹
Each plane a hurtling javelin of winged ordnance,
Bristle the heights above a screeching gale to hover;
Surely no eye that Sunward Escadrille can cover!⁴⁰ 105
There, meaningful, fledged as the Pleiades⁴¹

36. "Heaven's plumed side" is densely allusive. The phrase refers simultaneously to cloud cover, described two lines later as the "downy offings" masking the ferocity of war; to the winged forms of angels in the Christianized version of Ptolemaic astronomy; to an apostrophe in Whitman's "Passage to India" ("Passage to more than India! / Are thy wings plumed indeed for such far flights?; l. 420); to the plume of Hector's helmet in *The Iliad*, especially in book 6, where the plumed helmet frightens Hector's infant son; and to the plumed serpent who represents Quetzalcoatl, the Aztec god invoked in "The Dance."

37. "War's fiery kennel" plays both on the phrase "the dogs of war," from Shakespeare's *Julius Caesar* (3.1.273) but long since proverbial, and on "dogfight" as a term for close aerial combat.

38. The grenades blossom as their explosion shatters them into the "petals" of their expanding fragments; the image reverses the mythological transformation of a youth's spilled blood into a flower (from Hyacinthus to the hyacinth, Adonis to the anemone). The "sharp theorems" combine mental and physical injury, like the earlier "ammoniac proverbs."

39. Tellurian: earth born or earth dwelling; from Tellus, the Roman earth goddess. Fighter squadrons in World War I typically began operations at first light.

40. To untangle the grammar of the four-line sentence: the planes (Tellurian, that is, earth born wind-sleuths) are hurled like javelins at the sky above the gale; they hit home as if the sky were a shield and quiver like bristles, the shafts of the javelins, but at an altitude and an attitude toward the sun that removes them from sight, so that—surely!—no eye can cover them. *Escadrille* is French for a squadron of warplanes; prior to America's entry into World War I in 1917, a group of thirty-eight American aviators served in the most famous of these, the all-American Lafayette Escadrille.

41. The Pleiades, also known as the Seven Sisters, is a star cluster said to be chased across the sky by the hunter Orion. The cluster is in the constellation Taurus, adjacent to Orion in the winter sky in the Northern hemisphere. In classical mythology, Orion's pursuit led the gods to metamorphose the sisters first into doves and then into stars. The planes, fledged— that is, winged, like the Pleiades—undergo a similar metamorphosis from their Tellurian forms; "fledging," in the sense of feathering an arrow, extends the metaphor of the warplane as a javelin.

With razor sheen they zoom each rapid helix!
Up-chartered choristers of their own speeding
They, cavalcade on escapade, shear Cumulus—
Lay siege and hurdle Cirrus down the skies![42]   110
While Cetus-like, O thou Dirigible, enormous Lounger[43]
Of pendulous auroral beaches,[44]—satellited wide
By convoy planes, moonferrets that rejoin thee[45]
On fleeing balconies as thou dost glide,
—Hast splintered space!

                      Low, shadowed of the Cape,   115
Regard the moving turrets! From grey decks
See scouting griffons[46] rise through gaseous crepe
Hung low . . . until a conch of thunder answers
Cloud-belfries, banging, while searchlights, like fencers,
Slit the sky's pancreas of foaming anthracite[47]   120
Toward thee, O Corsair of the typhoon,[48]—pilot, hear!

42. Cirrus clouds form at higher altitudes than cumulus clouds; the planes cut through ("shear") the cumulus and rise above the cirrus, which they thus seem to hurtle (not Crane's "hurdle") down the skies. As they noisily spiral aloft ("up-chartered choristers" that "zoom each rapid helix"), the planes seek to conquer space by reaching the zenith, the high point of the imaginary sphere on which the heavenly bodies appear to be projected.

43. Like Hamlet's famous cloud, the dirigible resembles a whale; the comparison suggests a large rigid airship with full skeleton, that is, a zeppelin. Cetus, the Whale, is a large northern constellation named for the sea monster to whom, in classical mythology, the king of Ethiopia abandoned his daughter Andromeda; she was rescued by Perseus, who killed the monster. During World War I the Germans used zeppelins as bombers.

44. "Auroral beaches" may refer to the Northern Lights, the aurora borealis, or more generally—since the auroras are usually visible only from northern latitudes—to the colors of the sky at dawn, consistent with the "dawn patrol" alluded to earlier. Aurora was the Roman goddess of the dawn.

45. The surrounding convoy planes form the dirigible's satellites, metaphorically its moons, hence "moonferrets"; like ferrets, the planes are hunters.

46. Griffon: a mythological beast with the body of a lion and the head and wings of an eagle.

47. Anthracite: hard coal, which burns with intense heat. "Foaming anthracite" suggests a sky covered in billows of darkness from smoke, fog, or storm clouds, any of which may correspond to the "gaseous crepe" three lines earlier. The dark matter, slit open by the searchlights, is a kind of digestive fluid secreted by the "sky's pancreas" that threatens to dissolve and absorb the planes. The bizarre image of lethal digestion is continued a few lines later by its antidote, the pilot's eyes "bicarbonated"—given bicarbonate of soda for an upset stomach—by the plane's speed.

48. Corsair: a pirate or privateer, a swashbuckler; also the pirate's ship. The "Corsair of the typhoon" flies with the speed and strikes with the force of a hurricane at sea.

Thine eyes bicarbonated white by speed, O Skygak,[49] see
How from thy path above the levin's lance[50]
Thou sowest doom thou hast nor time nor chance
To reckon—as thy stilly eyes partake   125
What alcohol of space . . .! Remember, Falcon-Ace,[51]
Thou hast there in thy wrist a Sanskrit charge
To conjugate infinity's dim marge—
Anew . . .![52]

      But first, here at this height receive
The benediction of the shell's deep, sure reprieve!   130
Lead-perforated fuselage, escutcheoned wings
Lift agonized quittance, tilting from the invisible brink
Now eagle-bright, now

                quarry-hid, twist-

                    -ing, sink with

Enormous repercussive list-

                -ings down

Giddily spiralled

              gauntlets, upturned, unlooping   135
In guerilla sleights, trapped in combustion gyr-
Ing,[53] dance the curdled depth

            down whizzing

---

49. "Skygak," probably a misspelling of "skygack," pronounced "skyjack": Crane's coinage on the model of "steeplejack" to mean a worker or builder aloft; in a letter (to Waldo Frank, August 12, 1926), Crane says of his work on *The Bridge*: "I skip from one section to another now like a sky-gack or girder-jack."

50. "Levin": lightning.

51. An ace was an American fighter pilot in World War I who had least five confirmed aerial kills. The epithet "Falcon-Ace" recalls both the falcon of Hopkins's "The Windhover" (n. 32) and William Butler Yeats's "The Second Coming": "Turning and turning in the widening gyre, / The falcon cannot hear the falconer" (ll. 1–2).

52. "Sanskrit charge": the mandate, passed down through Whitman's "Passage to India," to render the conquest of space and time a means of interpreting the infinite:

O Soul, voyagest thou indeed on voyages like these?
Disportest thou on waters such as these?
Soundest below the Sanscrit and the Vedas?
Then have thy bent unleash'd.

Passage to you, your shores, ye aged fierce enigmas! . . .
You, strew'd with wrecks of skeletons that, living, never reach'd you. (ll. 226–32)

To "conjugate infinity's dim marge [shore, margin]" is both to spell out its forms of expression and to unite with it.

53. "Gyr-ing" reiterates the echo of Yeats's "The Second Coming."

Zodiacs, dashed
   (now nearing fast the Cape!)
      down gravitation's
       vortex into crashed
. . . . dispersion . . . into mashed and shapeless debris. . . .
By Hatteras bunched the beached heap of high bravery![54] 140

     *   *   *

The stars have grooved our eyes with old persuasions
Of love and hatred, birth,—surcease of nations . . .
But who has held the heights more sure than thou
O Walt!—Ascensions of thee hover in me now
As thou at junctions elegiac, there, of speed   145
With vast eternity, dost wield the rebound seed![55]
The competent loam, the probable grass,[56]—travail
Of tides awash the pedestal of Everest, fail
Not less than thou in pure impulse inbred
To answer deepest soundings![57] O, upward from the dead 150
Thou bringest tally, and a pact, new bound

54. This section merges the crash of a warplane shot down in combat (ironically "reprieved" by a shell that leaves its fuselage "lead-perforated") into the history of wrecks both by sea and air at Cape Hatteras. The falling plane, a modern image of Icarus, passes on a long arc along whizzing Zodiacs to end as debris in the waters of the cape, now a symbolic locale marking the grave of any "high bravery." "Gravitation's vortex" suggests a whirlpool (another widening gyre), which in combination with the promontory of Cape Hatteras yields a latter-day version of the monsters Scylla and Charybdis, predators of the hill and whirlpool, who present Homer's Odysseus with an insoluble problem on his voyage home: to avoid one danger is to risk the other.

55. The "junctions elegiac" of speed and infinity are heroic falls like the crash just recounted. Whitman, whose flight is mental rather than physical, holds the heights more surely and thus embodies and transmits a perennial principle of "ascension," or spiritual rebirth.

56. An allusion to Whitman's *Leaves of Grass*, specifically, perhaps, to section 6 of "Song of Myself," where Whitman "wield[s] the rebound seed" by taking the grass as an object of multiple interpretations, eventually resolving on it as a sign of both poetic and cosmic immortality. The grass blades are "so many uttering tongues" sprouting from the mouths of the dead; "The smallest sprout shows there is really no death, / And if ever there was it led forward life" (ll. 119, 126–27).

57. The travail of tides, although no less inbred in pure impulse than Whitman, fail, where he succeeds, in answering deepest soundings. Whitman's ascensions reverse the descents of the dead.

Of living brotherhood![58]

Thou, there beyond—

Glacial sierras and the flight of ravens,

Hermetically past condor zones,[59] through zenith havens

Past where the albatross has offered up   155

His last wing-pulse, and downcast as a cup

That's drained, is shivered back to earth[60]—thy wand

Has beat a song, O Walt,—there and beyond!

And this, thine other hand, upon my heart

Is plummet ushered of those tears that start   160

What memories of vigils, bloody, by that Cape,—[61]

58. In *Drum-Taps*, a collection of Civil War poems originally published apart from *Leaves of Grass*, Whitman recurrently tallies the war dead and vows to memorialize them. At the same time, he finds in the end of the war a pact of new brotherhood based on his conception of eroticized "manly love." See "Out of the Carnage Rose a Prophetic Voice," originally placed in "Calamus," the section of *Leaves* devoted to this theme:

> affection shall solve the problems of freedom yet,
> Those who love each other shall become invincible
>
> . . . .
> One from Massachusetts will be a Missourian's comrade
>
> . . . .
> It shall be customary in the houses and streets to see manly affection,
> The dauntless and rude shall touch face to face lightly,
> The dependence of Liberty shall be lovers. (ll. 2–3, 8, 14–16)

59. Ravens and condors are both carrion birds; ravens traditionally feast on the bodies of those fallen in battle; condors inhabit high mountains.

60. The albatross alludes primarily to the innocent creature in Samuel Taylor Coleridge's "The Rime of the Ancient Mariner." Coleridge's albatross flies alongside a ship of polar exploration as a good omen (thus making his wing pulse an offering), only to be senselessly shot down by an arrow from the protagonist's crossbow. The allegorical resonance with the crucifixion, explicit in Coleridge's text, echoes here in the image of the drained cup, recalling Jesus' agony in the Garden of Gethsemane and its culminating prayer of resignation: "O my Father, if this cup may not pass away from me, except I drink it, thy will be done" (Matthew 26:42); "Father . . . take away this cup from me; nevertheless, not what I will, but what thou wilt" (Mark 14:36). There may also be a secondary allusion to Charles Baudelaire's "The Albatross" ("L'Albatros"), in which the bird, an explicit symbol of the poet, is trapped by the sailors whose voyage it accompanies. Graceful in the air, the albatross is clumsy and ashamed on deck, where the sailors mock it: "The poet is the twin of this prince of the clouds, / Who haunts the tempest and laughs at archers; / Exiled on the ground amid the hooting crowd, / His giant wings impede his every step" (my translation).

61. The poet by the cape—the "ghoul mound" incarnating "fraternal massacre"—feels his heart struck by Whitman's "other," wartime hand as by a leaden plumb bob. The shock causes him to share Whitman's memories of bloody vigils and at the same time extends them beyond their origins in the Civil War. The vigils may refer either to the elder poet's work as a hospital volunteer during the Civil War or to his poem "Vigil Strange I Kept on the Field One Night," from *Drum-Taps*:

> Vigil strange I kept on the field one night;
> When you my son and my comrade dropt at my side that day,

Ghoul-mound of man's perversity at balk
And fraternal massacre! Thou, pallid there as chalk
Hast kept of wounds, O Mourner, all that sum[62]
That then from Appomattox stretched to Somme.[63]   165

Cowslip and shad-blow, flaked like tethered foam
Around bared teeth of stallions,[64] bloomed that spring
When first I read thy lines, rife as the loam
Of prairies, yet like breakers cliffward leaping!
O, early following thee, I searched the hill   170
Blue-writ and odor-firm with violets, 'til
With June the mountain laurel broke through green

> One look I but gave which your dear eyes return'd with a look I
>   shall never forget,
> One touch of your hand to mine O boy, reach'd up as you lay on the
>   ground,
> Then onward I sped in the battle, the even-contested battle,
> Till late in the night reliev'd to the place at last again I made my
>   way,
> Found you in death so cold dear comrade, found your body son of
>   responding kisses, (never again on earth responding,)
> Bared your face in the starlight, curious the scene, cool blew the
>   moderate night-wind,
> Long there and then in vigil I stood, dimly around me the
>   battlefield spreading,
> Vigil wondrous and vigil sweet there in the fragrant silent night. (ll. 3–10)

62. In "The Wound-Dresser," from *Drum-Taps*, Whitman assumes the role of a perennial mourner, continually reliving in dreams the care he gave in the hospitals to mortally wounded soldiers. He recalls the wounds in vivid physical detail ("I undo the clotted lint, remove the slough, wash off the matter and blood"), as if to preserve each one in memory.

63. The Civil War ended on April 9, 1865, when Robert E. Lee surrendered his army to Ulysses S. Grant at Appomattox Court House, Virginia. Appomattox was not the scene of a battle, but it serves here to encapsulate the "fraternal massacre" that was and remains by far the bloodiest war in American history, with over six hundred thousand dead. The same casualty figure attaches *on each side* of the battle of the Somme (July–November 1916), which the British Prime Minister Lloyd George called "The most gigantic, tenacious, grim, futile and bloody fight ever waged in the history of war." The Somme is a prime example of "man's perversity at balk"; when it was over, the Western allies had gained seven miles of territory against the Germans, a result of no strategic significance whatever.

64. The stallion may derive from section 32 of Whitman's "Song of Myself:

> A gigantic beauty of a stallion, fresh and responsive to my caresses,
> Head high in the forehead, wide between the ears,
> Limbs glossy and supple, tail dusting the ground,
> Eyes full of sparkling wickedness, ears finely cut, flexibly moving.
>
> His nostrils dilate as my heels embrace him,
> His well-built limbs tremble with pleasure as we race around and return.

The implied metaphor equates Whitman's sensuous pleasure in riding the stallion with Crane's in reading Whitman's lines.

And filled the forest with what clustrous sheen![65]
Potomac lilies,—then the Pontiac rose,[66]
And Klondike edelweiss of occult snows![67]   175

White banks of moonlight came descending valleys—
How speechful on oak-vizored palisades,[68]
As vibrantly I following down Sequoia alleys
Heard thunder's eloquence through green arcades
Set trumpets breathing in each clump and grass tuft—'til   180
Gold autumn, captured, crowned the trembling hill![69]

Panis Angelicus![70] Eyes tranquil with the blaze
Of love's own diametric gaze,[71] of love's amaze!

65. The laurel wreath is a classical symbol of victory in poetic (and athletic) competitions; Apollo was often depicted wearing a crown of laurel. The blossoming of the laurel corresponds to Crane's recognition of his poetic vocation as a result of first reading Whitman.

66. Whitman's "By Broad Potomac's Shore" seeks a source of poetry in a springtime pastoral similar to the one evoked in this segment:

> Again the freshness and the odors, again Virginia's summer sky, pellucid blue and silver,
> Again the forenoon purple of the hills,
> Again the deathless grass, so noiseless soft and green,
> Again the blood-red roses blooming.
> Perfume this book of mine O blood-red roses! (ll. 4–8)

67. "Occult snows" refers to the color of the edelweiss. The conjunction of place and flower names in this and the previous line, like the reference to "Sequoia alleys" two lines below, identifies the movement of Whitman's lines with traversal of the continent, a trope favored by Whitman himself.

68. The spaces between the oaks lining the cliff face (the palisade) suggest the slits of a visor, continuing the eye imagery that will return strongly at the start of the next section. The scene is "speechful," as the thunder two lines below is "eloquent," perhaps because in ancient religions the oak was sacred to gods who spoke in thunder, including Zeus/Jupiter, Thor/Donner, and their equivalent among the Druids, whose ceremonies were conducted in oak groves. The sacred oak is a key term in Frazer's *Golden Bough*, which Crane (as noted in "The Dance") knew well.

69. The breathing trumpets of autumn recall Shelley's "Ode to the West Wind," which links the wind's onset with the sound of thunder and concludes by fusing the rush of the west wind, the "breath of Autumn's being," with both the poet's utterance and the trumpet proclaiming resurrection in 1 Corinthians 15:52. Shelley, addressing the wind: "Be through my lips to unawakened earth / The trumpet of a prophecy!" (ll. 68–69). He echoes 1 Corinthians: "In a moment, in the twinkling of an eye, at the last trump: for the trumpet shall sound, and the dead shall be raised."

70. *Panis Angelicus* ("Bread of Angels"): the penultimate stanza of a communion hymn written by St. Thomas Aquinas for the Feast of Corpus Christi. The stanza has often been set to music as an independent poem; César Franck wrote an especially famous setting that Crane might have known. The stanza begins: "Panis angelicus / fit panis hominum; / dat panis coelicus / figuris terminum, / O res mirabilis! [Bread of angels / makes bread for humankind; / the heavenly bread / puts an end to symbols, / O wondrous thing!; my translation]." The appellation renders Whitman's body, or the body of his verse, a poetic Eucharist.

71. "Love's diametric gaze" probably refers to the mutual mirroring of each lover's image in the other's eye, a traditional trope best known through John Donne's poem "The Good-

Not greatest, thou,—not first, nor last,—but near
And onward yielding past my utmost year.   185
Familiar, thou, as mendicants in public places;
Evasive—too—as dayspring's spreading arc to trace is:—
Our Meistersinger,[72] thou set breath in steel;
And it was thou who on the boldest heel
Stood up and flung the span on even wing   190
Of that great Bridge, our Myth, whereof I sing![73]

Years of the Modern![74] Propulsions toward what capes?
But thou, *Panis Angelicus*, has thou not seen
And passed that Barrier that none escapes—
But knows it leastwise as death-strife?[75]—O, something green, 195

Morrow," which is also resonant with the geographical imagery of Crane's text: "My face in
thine eye, thine in mine appears, / And true plaine hearts doe in the faces rest, / Where can
we finde two better hemispheres / Without sharpe North, without declining West?" (ll. 15–
18). The diametric gaze may recapture the Edenic tranquility of "Hesperus mirrored in the
lucid pool" (l. 31 above; see n. 13).

72. Meistersinger ("master-singer"): a member of an artisans' guild in German cities of
the fourteenth through sixteenth centuries, who composed both lyric verses and melodies by
which to sing them. The Meistersingers are best known today, as they were in Crane's day,
through Richard Wagner's 1867 opera *Die Meistersinger*. The opera deals (among other things)
with the passing on of art from an older generation that preserves it to a younger generation
that transforms it. Wagner's protagonist, Walther von Stolzing, receives his artistic vocation
at the hands of an elder master, Hans Sachs (unlike Walther, a historical figure); the opera
culminates with the "prize song" by which Walther wins both entry into the guild and his
bride. Crane here stands to Whitman as Walther stands to Sachs.

73. Whitman "flung the span" of the Brooklyn Bridge by anticipating its symbolic power—
uniting space and time, past and present, self and other, history and myth—in "Crossing
Brooklyn Ferry." The "even wing" belongs to Whitman's seagulls, precursors of the solitary
gull in Crane's "To Brooklyn Bridge," whose wings "dip and pivot him" over the harbor: "I
too many and many a time cross'd the river of old, / Watched the Twelfth Month sea-gulls,
saw them high in the air floating with motionless wings, oscillating their bodies, / Saw how
the glistening yellow lit up parts of their bodies and left the rest in strong shadow, / Saw the
slow-wheeling circles and the gradual edging toward the south" (ll. 28–31).

74. "Years of the Modern": a poem by Whitman that celebrates advances in technology
(and thus "set[s] breath in steel") and ecstatically anticipates the still "unperform'd" future:
"No one knows what will happen next, such portents fill the days and nights; / Years propheti-
cal! the space ahead as I walk, as I vainly try to pierce it, is full of phantoms, / Unborn deeds,
things soon to be, project their shapes around me" (ll. 24–26).

75. This and the previous line echo Tennyson's valedictory poem "Crossing the Bar":

And may there be no moaning of the bar
    When I put out to sea,

But such a tide as moving seems asleep,
    Too full for sound and foam,
When that which drew from out the boundless deep
    Turns again home. (ll. 3–8)

The bar, Crane's "Barrier," is a ridge of shifting sand between the shore and the sea; shallow

Beyond all sesames of science was thy choice[76]
Wherewith to bind us throbbing with one voice,
New integers of Roman, Viking, Celt—
Thou, Vedic Caesar, to the greensward knelt![77]

And now, as launched in abysmal cupolas of space,[78]   200
Toward endless terminals, Easters of speeding light—
Vast engines outward veering with seraphic grace
On clarion cylinders pass out of sight[79]
To course that span of consciousness thou'st named
The Open Road[80]—thy vision is reclaimed!   205
What heritage thou'st signalled to our hands!

And see! the rainbow's arch[81]—how shimmeringly stands
Above the Cape's ghoul-mound, O joyous seer!
Recorders ages hence, yes, they shall hear
In their own veins uncancelled thy sure tread   210

---

sandbars stretch as far as fourteen miles offshore at Cape Hatteras, where they posed a serious danger to sailing ships. "Leastwise" in this passage means "least of all," not "at least."

76. "Something green": both the leaves of grass in common nature and the pages—leaves—of *Leaves of Grass.*

77. The poet kneeling to the grassland models conquest without violence, in contrast to the martial Vikings, Celts, and Romans; he is a "Vedic" Caesar, completing the passage (back) to India via texts of wisdom rather than acts of force.

78. "Abysmal cupolas": fathomless domes, representing both the imaginary form of the heavens and a latter-day version of Shelley's "Life, like a dome of many-colored glass / Stains the white radiance of eternity" ("Adonais," ll. 462–63). "Abysmal" is Crane's mistaken usage for "abyssal." The abyss here connotes infinite height rather than (or as equivalent to) infinite depth. A secondary meaning of "cupola," a cylindrical furnace for melting iron, comports with the poem's earlier emphasis on mechanical combustion.

79. Clarion: a medieval trumpet with a clear, shrill tone, associated in iconography with the music of the heavenly hosts and especially with the trumpet of resurrection (hence the "Easters of speeding light"). The cylinders are clarions because the planes are angelic—and because the engines are noisy.

80. In "Song of the Open Road," Whitman takes walking the public road as a complex symbol for endless physical, geographical, and spiritual exploration; Crane glosses the symbol here both literally, transferring it to the soaring movement of the planes beyond the limits of vision, and figuratively, as a "span," that is, a bridge, or what "To Brooklyn Bridge" calls a "curveship," of consciousness.

81. The rainbow, earlier invoked with the compound epithet "dayspring's spreading arc," assumes its biblical meaning as a sign of God's covenant after the Flood; the image is in keeping with the storm-wracked setting of Cape Hatteras: "And it shall come to pass, when I [God] bring a cloud over the earth, that the bow shall be seen in the cloud; and I will remember my covenant, which is between me and you and every living creature of all flesh; and the waters shall no more become a flood to destroy all flesh" (Genesis 9:14–15).

And read thee by the aureole 'round thy head[82]
Of pasture-shine,[83] *Panis Angelicus!*

                                   yes, Walt,
Afoot again, and onward without halt,—
Not soon, nor suddenly,—no, never let go
     My hand
          in yours,[84]
               Walt Whitman—
                    so—

82. In "Crossing Brooklyn Ferry," Whitman describes the recurrent experience of seeing his image in the water surrounded by a halo, as if he were a figure in a religious painting come to life, deified in purely naturalistic terms: "[I] had my eyes dazzled by the shimmering track of beams, / Look'd at the fine centrifugal spokes of light round the shape of my head in the sunlit water" (ll. 32–33).

83. The odd phrase "aureole . . . of pasture-shine" either misuses "pasture" as a synonym for "pastoral," in the sense both of idyllic nature and priestly care, or suggests a further reflection in a pool amid fertile land.

84. The image of men holding hands is a favorite of Whitman's and a leading motif in the "Calamus" poems. It also appears in two of the longer poems Crane cites here, "Crossing Brooklyn Ferry" ("What gods can exceed these that clasp me by the hand, and with voices I love call me promptly and loudly?"; l. 94) and "Song of the Open Road":

> Camerado, I give you my hand!
> I give you my love more precious than money,
> I give you myself before preaching or law;
> Will you give me yourself? will you come travel with me?
> Shall we stick by each other as long as we live? (ll. 220–24)

V. THREE SONGS

The one Sestos, the other Abydos hight.

—*Marlowe*

EPIGRAPH: From Christopher Marlowe's unfinished epyllion (short epic) *Hero and Leander* (1593). "Hight" means "named." Sestos and Abydos were towns on either side of the Helles- pont (today's Dardanelles), separating Hero, immured in a high tower, from her doomed lover. Marlowe's text combines the motifs of idealized romantic quest and sexually explicit, sometimes bawdy, entertainment; Crane's "Three Songs" do the same. The image of the tower carries over from the shapes of waves in "Ave Maria" to the "Cyclopean towers" of "The Harbor Dawn" to the Woolworth Building in "Virginia," the last of the "Three Songs." "Three Songs" are also loosely indebted to the three songs of the Thames Maidens in part 3, "The Fire Sermon," of Eliot's *The Waste Land*.

I wanted you, nameless Woman of the South,[1]
No wraith,[2] but utterly—as still more alone
The Southern Cross takes night
And lifts her girdles from her, one by one—[3]
High, cool,
       wide from the slowly smoldering fire   5
Of lower heavens,—
            vaporous scars![4]

Eve! Magdalene!
     or Mary, you?[5]

SOUTHERN CROSS: The constellation Crux, visible in the Southern Hemisphere most of the year. The poem follows the Cross as it traverses the night sky from dusk until dawn.

1. The Woman of the South is another mythical/cosmological incarnation of the Pocahontas-Muse figure central to *The Bridge*. Crane invokes her with a compressed but classically analogical simile: the speaker is to the Woman as the Southern Cross is to the night (traditionally personified as feminine). The simile is a more distanced form of the metaphor from "To Brooklyn Bridge": "And we have seen night lifted in thine arms." The motion of the constellation unveils the Woman's form but not her name, and she retains her "namelessness" (l. 22) even after the poet has settled (for the time being) on "Eve." The Southern Cross figures here not only as a stellar body and Christian symbol but also as a celestial lamp to guide a voyage by sea—a cosmological version of the lamp in Hero's tower. The Southern hemisphere lacks a readily visible pole star by which to navigate; the stars at the foot and the tip of the Southern Cross are customarily used instead.

2. The speaker insists that the woman he seeks is not a wraith—specifically, not a spectral product of sexual fantasy; see l. 27—but someone of flesh and blood. "Three Songs" progresses from the lack of any such person in "Southern Cross" to a travesty of her in "National Winter Garden" to an encounter with her in "Virginia."

3. The Southern Cross leads the night upwards toward the zenith, removing the veils ("girdles," wrappings, with a play on celestial meridians) of darkness until the five stars of the constellation have appeared one by one. The image of a celestial striptease anticipates the burlesque show of "National Winter Garden," while the ascent from the lower to the higher heavens anticipates the high tower of "Virginia."

4. The "vaporous scars" are probably the streaks of the Milky Way surrounding the constellation. The movement from a lower heaven (linked with "smoldering fire," presumably lust) to a higher one may recall the classical division of the goddess of love into lower and higher personae, an earthly Venus inciting sexual passion and a heavenly Venus embodying divine intelligence.

5. The three names ventured here for the nameless Woman correspond to the women evoked successively by the three songs. Crane assumes the traditional (but almost certainly erroneous) identification of Mary Magdalene, the disciple of Jesus who witnessed his crucifixion and discovered his resurrection, and the unnamed penitent sinner who anoints Jesus' feet in Luke 7:36–50. The figure of the Magdalene as prostitute or adulteress turned model penitent rose to prominence in the literature and especially the art of the middle ages and remained iconic throughout the twentieth century. The epithet "star of the sea" (from the

Whatever call, falls vainly on the wave.

O simian Venus,[6] homeless Eve,

Unwedded, stumbling gardenless to grieve[7]   10

Windswept guitars on lonely decks forever;[8]

Finally to answer all within one grave![9]

And this long wake of phosphor,[10]

                    iridescent

Furrow of all our travel—trailed derision!

Eyes crumble at its kiss. Its long-drawn spell   15

Latin hymn *Ave Maris Stella*) may hover in the background in the set-apart apostrophe to the Virgin Mary, whose name and persona will return in "Virginia."

6. The simian Venus is both a Darwinian throwback to primitive animality (an important motif in "National Winter Garden") and a reminder that apes were traditionally associated with unbridled desire.

7. Eve is both homeless and gardenless after the loss of Eden, for which misogynist tradition held her chiefly responsible. That she is unwedded may link her to the homeless squaw of "Indiana," who is forced to travel the long trail west on a stumbling jade.

8. "Windswept guitars": latter-day Aeolian harps. Linked by Crane to the form of the Bridge, the Aeolian harp symbolized the poetic imagination for Samuel Taylor Coleridge in "The Aeolian Harp" and "Dejection" and for William Wordsworth in *The Prelude*, 1: 41–47. The instrument—boxed strings stretched lengthwise over a sounding board between two supports—is laid flat on a window ledge, where its strings are randomly stirred by the wind. There may also be an ironic echo of Shelley's "With a Guitar, To Jane," where the guitar replaces the Aeolian harp, itself a surrogate for the fabled lyre of Apollo and Orpheus:

>   beneath Heaven's fairest star,
> The artist wrought this loved Guitar;
> And taught it justly to reply
> To all who question skillfully
> In language gentle as thy own. (ll. 57–61)

Crane may be alluding further to the numerous guitars and other stringed instruments in the Cubist still lifes painted by Braque and Picasso in and after 1907; the geometrical fragmentation of the image, for which music was a metaphor, was widely taken to mark a breakdown of traditional modes of perception. A similar possible referent is Picasso's more pictorial *Old Man with Guitar*, in which the exhaustion of the lyre-harp-guitar image seems complete; the painting is often considered the pictorial basis of Wallace Stevens's long poem of 1937, *The Man with the Blue Guitar*.

9. In Genesis 3:19–20, Adam names his wife Eve ("because she is mother of all living") immediately after God has told the couple that their disobedience has rendered them mortal—along, therefore, with all their progeny.

10. The long wake of phosphor is the luminescence at sea sometimes produced when the water is disturbed, as in the wake of a ship. Now known to be caused by living microorganisms, the luminescent sea was once thought to be caused by phosphorus and therefore to be a kind of liquid fire. It was superstitiously associated with suffering souls or evil spirits. Crane here may be reworking a famous passage from Samuel Taylor Coleridge's *Rime of the Ancient Mariner*: "About, about, in reel and rout / The death-fires danced at night; / The water, like a witch's oils, / Burnt green, and blue, and white" (ll. 127–30).

Incites a yell. Slid on that backward vision.[11]
The mind is churned to spittle, whispering hell.[12]

I wanted you . . . The embers of the Cross[13]
Climbed by aslant and huddling aromatically.
It is blood to remember; it is fire   20
To stammer back[14] . . . It is
God—your namelessness.[15] And the wash—

All night the water combed you with black
Insolence.[16] You crept out simmering, accomplished.
Water rattled that stinging coil, your   25

Rehearsed hair—docile, alas, from many arms.[17]
Yes, Eve—wraith of my unloved seed.[18]

11. "Backward vision": compare "the dark backward / and abysm of time" from Shakespeare's *The Tempest* (1.2.49–50), as well as "Cape Hatteras": "a labyrinth submersed / Where each sees only his dim past reversed" (ll. 30–31).

12. Compare Milton's Satan: "The mind is its own place, and in itself / Can make a heaven of hell, a hell of heaven" (*Paradise Lost*, 1: 254–55); also Marlowe, *Dr. Faustus*: "*Faustus*: How comes it then that thou art out of hell? *Mephistophilis*: Why, this is hell, nor am I out of it" (1.3.73–74).

13. "The embers of the Cross" refers to the Coalsack, a dark nebula bordering the Southern Cross. Clearly visible as an opaque patch intruding into the Southern Milky Way, the Coalsack appears beneath and slightly behind the Cross and thus follows it like a shadow across the night sky. The poem imagines the Coalsack as smoldering with the ashes of thwarted desire.

14. Lines 20–23 seek a way out of the smoldering abyss by linking the namelessness of the Woman with figures of increasingly mystical union with the divine: communion ("It is blood to remember"), the Pentecostal "tongues like as of fire," which descend on the Apostles of Christ so that "they were all filled with the Holy Ghost, and began to speak with other tongues, as the Spirit gave them utterance" (Acts 2:4); and direct theophany.

15. Crane here inverts the basic precept of negative theology, an important strain of both Neo-Platonic and Christian mysticism (among other traditions), which holds that God transcends finite understanding, so that nothing can be said about him except by negation. In negative theology the divine is nameless; in "Southern Cross," the nameless is divine.

16. Compare Eliot, "The Love Song of J. Alfred Prufrock": "I have heard the mermaids singing, each to each . . . / I have seen them riding seaward on the waves, / Combing the white hair of the waves blown back" (ll. 124, 125–26).

17. The image of a woman's dangerously seductive "rehearsed hair" was in wide circulation among artists and poets in the late nineteenth and early twentieth centuries. Crane's imagery suggests several frequent types: long locks "rehearsed" in the mirrors of coquettes, actresses, or prostitutes; flowing by water from nymphs, naiads, bathers, or Prufrock-like mermaids (n. 16); and adorning the bodies of femmes fatales in serpentine forms recalling both Eve (whose traditional iconography included what Milton calls her "wanton ringlets") and Medusa. Compare Eliot's "The Waste Land": "A woman drew her long black hair out tight / And fiddled whisper music on those strings" ("What the Thunder Said," ll. 377–78).

18. That the seed is "unloved" may suggest a scene of masturbation; the biblical image of wasting seed by spilling it on the ground (Genesis 38:9) may hover in the background, along

The Cross, a phantom, buckled—dropped below the dawn.
Light drowned the lithic[19] trillions of your spawn.

with an identification of the "seed," that is, semen, with the sea foam from which Venus was born. The speaker voices a heterosexual complaint in keeping with the poem's presiding imagery of mystical erotic union with the archetypal body of Pocahontas. Crane's homosexuality, articulated elsewhere in the poem (especially in "Cape Hatteras"), remains tacit here.

19. *Lithic* is a rare word and a strange one in this context. It means "stony," as if the sea surface had been flecked with stone; the reference is perhaps to the phosphorus (l. 13) once thought to cause the luminescence at sea. The closing lines describe the fading into dawn of the ocean's phosphorescence, which represents the "spawn" of Eve reinscribed as a sea-born goddess on the model of the earthly Venus, but in debased form and imbued with a Medusa-like power associated with the water's "stinging coil" (l. 25). The lines may also imply a mirror imaging between the phosphorescent sea and the stellar "trillions" of the Milky Way, both "drowned" by the light of dawn.

O utspoken buttocks[1] in pink beads
Invite the necessary cloudy clinch
Of bandy eyes. . . . No extra mufflings here:
The world's one flagrant, sweating cinch.[2]

And while legs waken salads in the brain[3]
You pick your blonde out neatly through the smoke.
Always you wait for someone else though, always—[4]
(Then rush the nearest exit through the smoke).

NATIONAL WINTER GARDEN: A burlesque theater operated by the Minsky brothers at Houston Street and Second Avenue on Manhattan's Lower East Side. Crane was a habitué, along with many other writers and artists of the era. The burlesque scene in the New York of the 1920s has been thoroughly documented by Gordon A. Tapper, to whose book *The Machine That Sings* many of the details in these notes are indebted. Tapper argues persuasively that traditional readings of "National Winter Garden" as a portrait of debased femininity, the latter-day corruption of Pocahontas, proceed from the mistaken assumption that Crane was repelled by burlesque. In fact, he was a fan, and enough of one to be noticed by Morton Minsky himself, who wrote of the family establishment that "We were getting a pretty classy clientele. . . . Regulars at that time included . . . the writers John Erskine and John Dos Passos [and] the columnist Walter Winchell. Such distinguished commentators as Robert Benchley . . . and George Jean Nathan were loyal attenders, as was a shy poet named Hart Crane, who wrote a poem in our honor" (69). Although a certain anxiety about the female body does haunt "National Winter Garden," much of the poem's apparently demeaning language has to be read as bawdily framed appreciation, a means of participating in the transgressiveness of the striptease. Many intellectuals of the period treated burlesque in these terms. The scene was also popular with homosexuals, perhaps because of its irreverent play with the trappings of gender and sexuality. Part of that play involved comic rhyming, a patter that, as Tapper observes, Crane mimics in describing the performance.

    1. The use of "outspoken" to indicate the exposure of the dancer's buttocks is linked with the denial of "extra mufflings" two lines later to mark the exposure of her body more generally; her near nudity metaphorically becomes a form of candid speech, a ribald, burlesque version of the word made flesh.

    2. The cinch, literally a saddle belt, is the dancer's g-string. In circling her body, it identifies her flesh with the world, that is, with the globe, especially as circled by sailing ships or by the navigational lines of latitude and longitude. In another sense, this world of flesh is a "cinch" in the sense of easy success and sexual availability.

    3. "Salads in the brain" may echo the "salad days" of Shakespeare's Cleopatra, referring to her youthful affair with Julius Caesar (*Antony and Cleopatra*, 1.5), as well as Yeats's description of Aphrodite (with reference to his own inamorata, Maud Gonne): "It's certain that fine women eat / A crazy salad with their meat" ("A Prayer for My Daughter").

    4. Compare Eliot, from *The Waste Land*:

> Who is the third who walks always beside you?
> When I count, there are only you and I together
> But when I look ahead up the white road
> There is always another one walking beside you
> Gliding wrapt in a brown mantle, hooded

Always and last, before the final ring   9
When all the fireworks blare, begins
A tom-tom scrimmage with a somewhere violin,[5]
Some cheapest echo of them all—begins.

And shall we call her whiter than the snow?[6]
Sprayed first with ruby, then with emerald sheen[7]—
Least tearful and least glad (who knows her smile?)
A caught slide shows her sandstone grey between.[8]

Her eyes exist in swivellings of her teats,[9]   17
Pearls whip her hips, a drench of whirling strands
Her silly snake rings begin to mount, surmount
Each other[10]—turquoise fakes on tinseled hands.

> I do not know whether a man or a woman.
> ("What the Thunder Said," ll. 360–65)

5. The tom-tom simultaneously refers to the sound of Indian drums and to the drums in a jazz combo. The lines recall Eliot's "Among the windings of the violins,/ And the ariettes/ Of cracked cornets,/ Inside my brain a dull tom-tom begins" ("Portrait of a Lady," ll. 29–31).

6. Snowy whiteness was, of course, a clichéd image of female chastity; here the rhetorical question receives its answer—*No*—not simply because the dancer's chastity is moot but because the lighting effects that typically accompanied a striptease routine at Minsky's would "spray" her body with red and green light.

7. The image of the ruby recalls both the "scarlet woman" described in Revelation 17:3–4 as the Whore of Babylon and the virtuous women of Proverbs 31:10 whose "price is far above rubies." The emerald is traditionally associated with royalty.

8. The slide is a lighting mechanism used to highlight the stages of the striptease; the reference here to ruby and emerald sheen (lighting effects, as n. 6 observes) joins the biblical and poetic associations of the gems to a travesty that exposes the uncensored truth; the caught slide reveals the dancer's pubis as other than the fetishized surfaces surrounding it.

9. The equation between the dancer's exposed nipples and her eyes echoes Crane's response to a performance in 1922 by the controversial modernist dancer Isadora Duncan. For Crane, Duncan's exposure of her own breast in this high-art performance was an expression not of how her body was seen but of what her eye, and her mind's eye, could see (and, seeing, also say): "Glorious to see her there with her right breast and nipple quite exposed, telling the audience that the truth was not pretty, that it was really indecent, and telling them (boobs!) about Beethoven, Tschaikowsky [sic], and Scriabine" (to Gordon Munson, December 12, 1922). It is not clear whether "boobs" is a pun or whether Crane knew that the exposure of a single breast was an Amazonian pose. Crane did, however, repeat an association made by Duncan herself between her dance and the "Calamus" section of Whitman's *Leaves of Grass*. "Calamus" celebrates "manly love," and its citation suggests that avowals of hetero-and homosexual love are fundamentally congruent and even interchangeable.

10. The snake rings recall the eagle and the serpent of "The Dance," together with the traditional association of woman and the serpent based on the temptation of Eve. The image of a dancing snake charmer, part of the popular exoticism of "low" popular entertainment with carnival roots, is also in play, as well as the similar image of Salome, also a frequent figure in the popular culture of the time, whose dancing was frequently represented as writhing and serpentine. The mounting of the rings suggests a travesty, that is, a burlesque version of eternity, of which the snake that devours its own tail (the ouroboros) is a traditional symbol. The writhing pool is probably a euphemistic image for the vagina, to which the dancer's

We wait that writhing pool, her pearls collapsed,
—All but her belly buried in the floor;
And the lewd trounce of a final muted beat!
We flee her spasm through a fleshless door. . . .[11]

Yet, to the empty trapeze of your flesh,[12]   25
O Magdalene, each comes back to die alone.[13]
Then you, the burlesque of our lust—and faith,
Lug us back lifeward[14]—bone by infant bone.[15]

whole body is assimilated; it suggests a whirlpool, to which mermaids, most famously the Lorelei, would lure sailors to destruction. The collapse into the writhing pool, eagerly anticipated, suggests sexual climax, but at the same time presents the dancer's own orgasm as a traumatic spectacle: "We flee her spasms through a fleshless door." The womb, traditionally the door of birth, undergoes a reversal in the image; it is fled for an unspecified "fleshless" (hence dead and insubstantial as well as immaterial) counterpart.

11. Although the dance has reached its orgasmic climax ("the lewd trounce of a final muted beat!"), it is an image not of union but of separation; the members of the audience, the poet among them, flee from the place of the exposed flesh. The "fleshless door" may echo Eliot's "Whispers of Immortality": "Webster was much possessed by death / And saw the skull beneath the skin / And breastless creatures underground / Leaned backwards with a lipless grin" (ll. 1–4).

12. The trapeze was a stage prop, like the poles used by nude dancers today; it was left over from the circus and was adopted in burlesque as a sexual appliance, a surrogate phallus or machine body, here merged with the flesh that swings the onlooker back from death to life, just as the prototype, Mary Magdalene, was the first witness of Christ's resurrection.

13. That each of us comes back to die alone recalls the "single grave" of "Southern Cross." In context it also plays on the archaic sexual meaning of *to die* as to come to orgasm, the "little death" or *petit mort*. The solitariness of this "death" also suggests masturbation, recalling the image of "unloved seed" in "Southern Cross."

14. "Lug us back lifeward": the first of two parodies (burlesques) by which the dancer as Magdalene conjoins "our lust—and faith." Here the woman who witnessed the empty tomb signaling the resurrection becomes the maternal womb/tomb through which we are drawn ("lugged") back to life, despite the dead weight of our spiritual decline. The phrasing may burlesque Hamlet's "I'll lug the guts into the neighbor room" (3.4).

15. The second parody casts the dancing Magdalene in the role of Jesus, with "us" in the role of Lazarus. The ambivalent linkage between sexual desire and a return to life is suggested by the phrase "bone by infant bone," which recalls the conjugal celebration of Genesis 2:23— "bone of my bones, flesh of my flesh"—and at the same time makes a bawdy play on male arousal: bone by bone, erection by erection.

6. The Woolworth Building, ca. 1916.

VIRGINIA

O rain at seven[1]
　Pay-check at eleven[2]—
Keep smiling the boss away,[3]
Mary (what are you going to do?)
Gone seven—gone eleven,　　　　　　　5
And I'm still waiting for you—

O blue-eyed Mary with the claret scarf,[4]
　Saturday Mary, mine[5]!

　It's high carillon
　From the popcorn bells![6]　　　　　　10

VIRGINIA: The title alludes to Queen Elizabeth I, the "Virgin Queen," for whom Virginia was named, and to Pocahontas, the chieftain's daughter born in the virgin territory that would become Virginia. The utopian (or half utopian) space of this poem, however, is urban and Bohemian: Lower Manhattan's Prince Street, in Soho, and Bleecker Street, which in Greenwich Village runs parallel to Prince. Both streets end at the Bowery, the heading of the drunken sailor in "Cutty Sark."

1. The regenerative rain of "Virginia" recapitulates and renders less equivocal the long-awaited rain in the closing section, "What the Thunder Said," of Eliot's *The Waste Land*; the sound of carillon bells in Crane, referred to below, replaces Eliot's rumble of "dry sterile thunder without rain."

2. "Seven" and "eleven" refer both to the principal dice throws in craps and to the half-day working hours that the poem's Mary has on Saturdays. As the poem suggests in its final lines, "Mary" is an office worker in the Woolworth Building on Lower Broadway, the "high tower" beneath which the speaker of the poem stands in the classic posture of the wooer who sings to his mistress as she stands on a balcony.

3. True to her name, Mary fends off her boss's persistent sexual advances. Her behavior makes her the antithesis of the typist "home at teatime" in Eliot's *The Waste Land* ("A Game of Chess"), who apathetically allows herself to be used sexually by a "young man carbuncular" because she is "bored and tired."

4. Mary's eyes have the Virgin's traditional color, and her claret scarf modestly sublimates the ruby sheen (and "scarlet" associations) of the dancer in "National Winter Garden."

5. The rhythm here and throughout suggests that of popular song, which the poem mimics or parodies; Susan Jenkins Brown suggests a specific source, "What Do You Do Sunday, Mary?" (or simply "Mary," lyrics by Irving Caesar, music by Stephen Jones) from the 1923 musical *Poppy*. The lyrics include the lines: "It's only Saturday that you can be found;/What do you do Mary, All week 'round?" Crane's echo of the question adapts it to the poem's evocation of a once-weekly "sabbatical" from long hours of work for low wages. The play, incidentally, starred W. C. Fields, to whom it gave the famous line "Never give a sucker an even break!"

6. The bells on the cart of a street vendor selling popcorn suggest the more elevated sound of a carillon: a series of bells set in a tower, played either by a keyboard or by a mechanism resembling a piano roll. The image of the carillon both recalls the tower of Hero and Leander alluded to in the epigraph of "Three Songs" and anticipates the tower invoked at the end of

Pigeons by the million—
And Spring in Prince Street
Where green figs gleam
By oyster shells!⁷

O Mary, leaning from the high wheat tower,⁸   15

Let down your golden hair!⁹

High in the noon of May
On the cornices of daffodils
The slender violets stray,¹⁰

"Virginia"; the sound of a mechanical instrument, although idyllic here, also echoes the more ominous pianola in "Cutty Sark."

7. Crane's gleaming Prince Street idyll reverses the dank cityscape of Eliot's "The Love Song of J. Alfred Prufrock": "The muttering retreats / Of restless nights in one-night cheap hotels / And sawdust restaurants with oyster shells" (ll. 5–7). The figs and oysters for sale on Prince Street suggest the abundance made briefly available by the "paycheck at eleven" and the freedom (however transient) of the weekend; both foodstuffs were thought to have aphrodisiac powers. In the Song of Solomon, green figs represent the awakening of love: "The fig tree putteth forth her green figs, and the vines with the tender grape give a good smell. Arise, my love, my fair one, and come away" (2:13). The "millions of pigeons" may similarly suggest the modern urban version of turtle doves, a traditional symbol of true love that, along with other images central to "Virginia," appears in the Song of Solomon immediately preceding the passage about the green figs: "The flowers appear on the earth; the time of the singing of birds is come, and the voice of the turtle is heard in our land" (2:12). As the next lines are about to concede, however, there is a certain fairy-tale quality about the entire scene.

8. The "high wheat tower" associates Mary with Pocahontas, who in "The Dance" "rose with the maize" and is hailed, a specifically American fertility goddess, as "immortal in the maize" (ll. 62, 64). The presentation of Mary in "Virginia" closely echoes Vachel Lindsay's portrayal of Pocahontas in "Our Mother Pocahontas" (1917):

> She sings of lilacs, maples, wheat,
> Her own soil sings beneath her feet,
> Of springtime
> And Virginia,
> Our Mother, Pocahontas.

9. At this point Pocahontas-Mary merges with Rapunzel, the long-haired heroine of the fairy tale retold by the Brothers Grimm. Sequestered, like Marlowe's Hero, in an isolated tower, Rapunzel lets down her golden hair to be used as a rope by her lover, a prince, who climbs to her hand over hand. Unlike Hero's and Leander's, however, their story—after many dark vicissitudes—has a happy ending. The gold of Rapunzel's hair merges with the gold of wheat sheaves to render the urban scene both legendary and pastoral.

10. Just as she has an emblematic color, the Virgin Mary has an emblematic month, which is May. The phrase "noon of May" associates the high point of the season with the sun's daily high point in the sky, a link that, in association with the solar gold of Mary-Rapunzel's hair, imports a cosmological value to the urban scene and links images of planetary order with everyday life, even integrating the crap-shooting gangs in Bleecker Street into the "shining" totality. Of the flowers mentioned by Crane, daffodils and violets recall famous passages of English Romantic poetry: the "host of golden daffodils" in Wordsworth's "I Wandered Lonely as a Cloud," the "violet by a mossy stone, / Half hidden from the eye" in his "She Dwelt among the Untrodden Ways," where the violet is a metaphor for a beloved woman

Crap-shooting gangs in Bleecker reign,[11]   20
Peonies with pony manes—[12]
Forget-me-nots at windowpanes:

Out of the way-up nickel-dime tower shine,[13]
        Cathedral Mary,
                Shine!—[14]

before her untimely death, and the "fast-fading violets covered up in leaves" of Keats's "Ode to a Nightingale." Forget-me-nots traditionally symbolize fidelity and true love.

11. The repeated reference to craps in the poem is somewhat puzzling; perhaps the idea is that Mary in her tower (who is, after all, just an ordinary young woman in a commercial building) represents the possibility of subordinating, rising above, a world of mere contingency to touch upon enduring forms and truths—at least on Saturday when the week's work is over at last.

12. The "pony manes" may suggest the lush heaviness of what Keats called "the wealth of globed Peonies" ("Ode on Melancholy," l. 17); Crane may be playing on the displaced eroticism of the image (followed immediately, in Keats, by the words "Or if thy mistress"). In the 1920s "pony" was slang for a burlesque dancer or chorus girl.

13. The phrase "nickel-dime tower" gives away the identity of the skyscraper/cathedral as the Woolworth Building, also known as the "Cathedral of Commerce" since its opening ceremony in 1913. At fifty-seven stories, it was intended to be the world's tallest building, a status it retained during the composition of *The Bridge*. (The Chrysler Building surpassed it in 1930.) F. W. Woolworth, who commissioned the building, was the head of a multi-million dollar chain of "Five-and- Ten-Cent Stores" popularly referred to as "Five and Dimes"—the Wal-Marts of their day. Woolworth stores were among the first to make their merchandise available for handling by customers; many of them had popular lunch counters. The company declined in the later twentieth century and reorganized itself as a seller of sporting goods, today's Foot Locker. The Woolworth Building is the poem's cathedral tower not only because of its sobriquet but also because its style is pseudo-gothic. Incidentally, the "nickel" in "nickel-dime tower" connects "Virginia" with both "Van Winkle" ("Keep hold of that nickel for car-change, Rip") and "Cutty Sark" ("the nickel-in-the-slot piano").

14. The injunction to shine invokes the golden halo surrounding the head of the Virgin in medieval and Renaissance art.

VI. QUAKER HILL

I see only the ideal. But no ideals
have ever been fully successful on
this earth.

—Isadora Duncan

The gentian weaves her fringes,
The maple's loom is red.

—Emily Dickinson

QUAKER HILL: This was the last section of *The Bridge* to be conceived and the last to be completed (in 1929). Quaker Hill is a hamlet in Pawling, New York, about seventy miles north of New York City, where Crane lived for a time in 1925. Pawling is the site of a Quaker meeting house, built in 1763; the poem uses it, along with a variety of other buildings, to register a steep cultural decline as corrupt pleasure seeking displaces the Quaker ideals of simplicity, peace, love, and community.

EPIGRAPHS: The first epigraph is from Isadora Duncan's 1927 autobiography, *My Life*, which Crane read in 1928 and found "a very sad but beautiful book." Duncan (1878–1927), whom Crane had admired in 1922 (see n. 9 of "National Winter Garden"), danced barefoot, with loose hair, in simple classical Greek dress. The fringed gentian in the second epigraph is a bright blue wildflower that blooms in the fall; the red of the maples also indicates the season in which "Quaker Hill" is set. Dickinson's poem is no. 21 in R. W. Franklin's *The Poems of Emily Dickinson*; only four lines long, it concludes, "My departing blossoms / Obviate parade," an internalization of regret as pertinent to Crane's text as the lines quoted in the epigraph. Crane may have been attracted by Dickinson's metaphor of weaving, which is resonant with his description of the cable strands of the Bridge.

Perspective never withers from their eyes;[1]
    They keep that docile edict of the Spring
That blends March with August Antarctic skies:
These are but cows that see no other thing
Than grass and snow, and their own inner being[2]
Through the rich halo that they do not trouble
Even to cast upon the seasons fleeting
Though they should thin and die on last year's stubble.

And they are awkward, ponderous and uncoy . . .   9
While we who press the cider mill,[3] regarding them—
We, who with pledges taste the bright annoy
Of friendship's acid wine, retarding phlegm,[4]
Shifting reprisals ('til who shall tell us when
The jest is too sharp to be kindly?) boast
Much of our store of faith in other men
Who would, ourselves, stalk down the merriest ghost.

1. "Their eyes": those of the cows in l. 4
2. The opening of the poem is a paraphrase of a famous passage from section 32 of Whitman's "Song of Myself":

> I think I could turn and live with the animals, they are so placid
>   and self-contain'd,
> I stand and look at them long and long.
> They do not sweat and whine about their condition,
> They do not lie awake in the dark and weep for their sins,
> They do not make me sick discussing their duty to God.
> Not one is dissatisfied, not one is demented with the mania of owning things. (ll. 683–89)

3. The cider mill recalls Keats's ode, "To Autumn": "Or by a cider-press, with patient look, / Thou watchest the last oozing hours by hours" (ll. 21–22). The watcher, unlike the cattle, contemplates the passing of time and the seasons, a topic raised Keats in language that Crane has echoed at the end of the preceding stanza:

> Where are the songs of Spring? Ay, where are they?
>   Think not of them, thou hast thy music too,—
> While barred clouds bloom the soft-dying day,
>   And touch the stubble plains with rosy hue;
> Then in a wailful choir the small gnats mourn
>   Among the river shallows. (ll. 23–28)

4. "Retarding phlegm": clearing the throat, presumably a sign of hypocrisy, before the toast made with "friendship's acid wine," the antithesis to the sweet apple cider, and holding back the phlegmatic temperament associated with the docility of the cows.

Above them old Mizzentop,[5] palatial white   17
Hostelry—floor by floor to cinquefoil dormer
Portholes the ceilings stack their stoic height.[6]
Long tiers of windows staring out toward former
Faces—loose panes crown the hill and gleam[7]
At sunset with a silent, cobwebbed patience . . .[8]
See them, like eyes that still uphold some dream
Through mapled vistas, cancelled reservations!

High from the central cupola, they say   25
One's glance could cross the borders of three states;[9]
But I have seen death's stare in slow survey
From four horizons that no one relates . . .[10]

5. "Old Mizzentop": properly Mizzen Top, named for a local peak, a palatial hotel in Quaker Hill from 1880 to 1933. According to an 1882 history of the locale, the hotel "command[s] an extensive view of mountain and valley scenery, and contains in all 145 rooms, 128 being used as sleeping apartments. The servants' departments are in a separate building containing sixteen rooms. The interior of the hotel is finished in the most modern style, and has all the conveniences of bath rooms, gas, steam heating apparatus, billiard room, bowling alleys, and telegraphic communication with New York." By the late 1920s, the hotel had been abandoned and was awaiting demolition. "Mizzentop" is also a nautical term recalling "Cutty Sark": a platform just above the head of the mizzen-mast of a sailing ship.

6. "Cinquefoil dormer / Portholes": a sign of wealth and elegance of design, now in decay. The dormers are windows projecting over the sloping roof of the hotel's top story; the cinquefoil is an arching or circular ornament consisting of five leaves.

7. "Panes" in this line and "tiers" in the preceding one are homophones for "pains" and "tears." Crane invests the hotel with the trappings of a haunted Gothic mansion, in particular, the decaying namesake of Edgar Allen Poe's story "The Fall of the House of Usher." The story includes a poem, "The Haunted Palace," that equates the staring eyes of the protagonist Roderick Usher with the windows of his house; at the end of the story, the house collapses into its own reflection in the pool at its base.

8. "Silent, cobwebbed patience": the cobwebs litter the deserted hotel. The phrase plays ironically on Whitman's lyric "A Noiseless Patient Spider," as if the idealized form of the spider's continuously woven web ("to explore the vacant vast surrounding, / It launched forth filament, filament, filament out of itself"; ll. 4–5) had given way to its dusty, abandoned counterpart, the cobweb. Whitman takes the spider as an image of the soul building a bridge of cable strands: "Ceaselessly musing, venturing, throwing, seeking the spheres to connect them, / Till the bridge you need will be formed, till the ductile anchor hold" (ll. 8–9). The empty stare of the hotel may represent *The Bridge* itself at an impasse as the poem tries to "uphold some dream / Through mapled vistas, cancelled reservations!"

9. New York, Massachusetts, and Connecticut.

10. The four horizons "that no one relates" are not geographical. Crane may be thinking of "death's stare" as following the course of the four rivers that converge at the center of the classical underworld: the Styx (the river of detestation), Phlegethon (the river of fire), Cocytus (the river of lamentation), and Acheron (the river of pain). The idea of a journey to the underworld is basic to the next section of the poem, "The Tunnel." Or the stare may carry an echo of Eliot's "The Hollow Men": "Eyes I dare not meet in dreams / In death's dream kingdom / These do not appear" (ll. 19–21). Or the fourfold stare may invert the blindness of the hooded, "Janus-visaged Shadow" of Shelley's *The Triumph of Life*: "All the four faces

Weekenders avid of their turf-won scores,
Here three hours from the semaphores,[11] the Czars
Of golf, by twos and threes in plaid plusfours[12]
Alight with sticks abristle and cigars.

This was the Promised Land,[13] and still it is   33
To the persuasive suburban land agent
In bootleg roadhouses where the gin fizz[14]
Bubbles in time to Hollywood's new love-nest pageant.[15]
Fresh from the radio in the old Meeting House
(Now the New Avalon Hotel[16]) volcanoes roar

of that charioteer / Had their eyes banded" (ll. 99–100). (The Roman Janus could have four faces as well as the more familiar two.)

11. Semaphores: a signalling device using hand-held flags. Semaphores are closely associated with sailing, so the implication is that the weekend golfers have torn themselves away from yacht races to play golf. They could no longer have played at Mizzen Top, but the Dutcher golf course would have been available; built in 1890 (and still operating today), it is the oldest nine-hole course in the United States.

12. Plusfours: the long, wide Knickerbocker trousers traditionally worn by golfers. The "Czars of golf" dress up for the game, carry elaborate sets of clubs (they "alight with sticks abristle"), and smoke cigars to celebrate their wealth and leisure.

13. Promised Land: the America of the Pilgrims and pioneers, a latter-day version of the land of Canaan promised by God to Abraham and his posterity in Genesis 12–13. The metaphor was a traditonal mainstay of American rhetoric, hymnody, and civic culture.

14. The gin fizz epitomizes drinking in roadhouses and speakeasies during the Prohibition era (1919–33). Crane, a prodigious drinker (he wrote much of his poetry while drunk) is not denouncing alcohol per se (or even dives; he liked those too) but the cheap "bathtub" gin that was the most widely consumed liquor during the period; the gin fizz was popular in part because its additional flavorings cut the taste of the bad gin. Crane's implication is that Prohibition travestied the Dionysian power of drink (see his poem "The Wine Menagerie"), reducing its consumption to something false and therefore sleazy, on a par with the real estate agent's pitching shabby suburban houses.

15. "Love-nest" was as ambiguous a term in the 1920s as it is today, with the contrary connotations of illicit affairs and cozy or sentimental romance. Sentiment prevailed in Louis Hirsch's popular song "The Love Nest," from the 1920 musical *Mary*:

Just a love nest
Cozy with charm . . .
Better than a palace with a gilded dome
Is a love nest
You can call home.

"Hollywood's new love-nest pageant" degrades fervent passion to sentimental escapism.

16. An exercise of poetic license: there was no such hotel in Pawling, and the meeting house is still standing. The hotel's pretentious Arthurian name points to a false paradise. Avalon was a medieval version of the classical Isles of the Blest, to which King Arthur was transported after receiving an apparently fatal wound in his final battle. According to legend, followed by the account in Tennyson's *Idylls of the King*, he would be healed and return again when needed most.

A welcome to highsteppers[17] that no mouse
Who saw the Friends[18] there ever heard before.

What cunning neighbors history has in fine![19]   41
The woodlouse[20] mortgages the ancient deal
Table that Powitzky[21] buys for only nine-
Ty-five at Adams' auction,[22]—eats the seal,
The spinster polish of antiquity . . .
Who holds the lease on time and on disgrace?
What eats the pattern with ubiquity?
Where are my kinsmen and the patriarch race?[23]

The resigned factions of the dead preside.   49
Dead rangers bled their comfort on the snow;
But I must ask slain Iroquois to guide
Me farther than scalped Yankees knew to go:[24]

17. "Highsteppers": hotel quests doing one of the era's energetic popular dances, such as the Charleston or Lindy Hop, which involved swinging, jumping, hugging, and grinding.

18. A member of the Society of Friends, that is, a Quaker. The mouse is proverbial: "poor as a church mouse," "quiet as a mouse."

19. Compare Eliot's "Gerontion": "Think now / History has many cunning passages, contrived corridors / And issues, deceived with whispering ambitions" (ll. 35–37).

20. Woodlice live under rocks and logs and feed on decaying plant matter, so the pest that defaces the "ancient deal table" is an imaginary creature; the name, not the bug, is what matters. Deal tables are made of soft woods such as fir or pine. Most are simple plank tables; Crane's reference to them may connote the (lost) plainness and simplicity of the Quaker heritage.

21. "Powitzky" is an invented name, meant to sound Polish and, with anti-Semitic venom, probably Jewish; Crane may have derived it from *Porwitsky*, the name of a Polish neighbor in Pawling. Powitsky's foiled bargain for the deal table is another sign of decline, as the antique American table falls into the hands of a Jewish huckster.

22. "Adams' auction" is an obvious pun on "Adam's auction," suggesting not simply the loss but the corrupted selling out of the former American Eden.

23. Crane's "kinsmen" comprise a group of distinguished families with roots in the colonial era; his ancestors emigrated to North America from England in 1645 and 1646; they participated in the Revolutionary War, the Civil War, and the westward trek to the Pacific. The "patriarch race" might refer to the country's Founding Fathers (Crane could even claim John Adams as a distant ancestor), but the ensuing stanza makes it more likely that the reference is to the Iroquois Indians, who would once have occupied the land that became Quaker Hill.

24. The Iroquois confederation consisted of the Cayuga, Mohawk, Oneida, Onondaga, and Seneca nations, joined in the eighteenth century by the Tuscarora. The parent group had been in existence since at least the sixteenth century. The Iroquois occupied territory in southern Ontario, Quebec, New York State, and Pennsylvania. Their confederation was notable for its sophisticated political organization, which included an orally transmitted constitution. It was, however, a casualty of the American Revolution, which split the member nations into pro-British and pro-American factions.

Shoulder the curse of sundered parentage,[25]
Wait for the postman driving from Birch Hill
With birthright by blackmail,[26] the arrant page
That unfolds a new destiny to fill. . . .

So, must we from the hawk's far stemming view,   57
Must we descend as worm's eye to construe[27]
Our love of all we touch, and take it to the Gate[28]
As humbly as a guest who knows himself too late,
His news already told? Yes, while the heart is wrung,
Arise—yes, take this sheaf of dust upon your tongue![29]
In one last angelus lift throbbing throat—[30]
Listen, transmuting silence with that stilly note

25. "The curse of sundered parentage" refers primarily to the violently divided legacy of Indian and white cultures—"slain Iroquois" and "scalped Yankees"—in the formation of national identity. But the phrase also introduces a personal digression. Crane's parents had divorced in 1917; his relationships with them were difficult at best, and he broke permanently with his mother in 1928 after she threatened to block his small inheritance from his grandmother. As he explained in a letter to Charlotte and Richard Rychtarik (February 26, 1929), "she threatened to do all sorts of things if I did not come at once [to her] in California and spend it [sic] with her—among which she said she would write to my father and try to get him to intercede with the bank against paying me!"

26. "Birthright by blackmail": the threats from Crane's mother. From the letter cited in the previous note: "[She] got people who were practically strangers to write me threatening and scolding letters, so that I never came home from work without wonder—and trembling about what I should find awaiting me." Birch Hill is a locality in Pawling; by 1929, the itinerant Crane received most of his mail via an address in the nearby town of Patterson.

27. The hawk and the worm are homely, deromanticized versions of the eagle and the serpent that preside over much of *The Bridge*. The descent from panorama to myopia anticipates the next section of the poem, "The Tunnel," which forms the modern equivalent of a classical descent into the underworld. Crane may be alluding to the hawk that famously appears at the head of the last section (no. 52) of Whitman's "Song of Myself": "The spotted hawk swoops by and accuses me, he complains of my gab and my loitering. // I too am not a bit tamed, I too am untranslatable. / I sound my barbaric yawp over the roofs of the world." The worm may have an allusive resonance beyond its proverbial association with death. In the "Book of Thel," William Blake (whom Crane greatly admired and who supplies the epigraph to "The Tunnel") wrote: "every thing that lives, / Lives not alone, nor for itself: fear not and I will call / The weak worm from its lowly bed, and thou shalt hear its voice" (2.26–28; the speaker is not a person but a "little Cloud . . . / Hovering and glittering on the air"; 2.6).

28. The Gate refers forward to the epigraph of "The Tunnel," from Blake's poem "Morning": "To Find the Western path / Right thro' the Gates of Wrath."

29. The oxymoronic "sheaf of dust" is the first of a series of paradoxes based on the idea of pain as a sacrament: the dust of mortality becomes the sheaf of the harvest; the "stilly note" of pain transmutes the silence; the whip-poor-will's song breaks the heart and saves it.

30. The *angelus*, the prayer commemorating the Incarnation introduced in "Ave Maria," returns here in parallel with the natural cycle of dawn, noon, and dusk. Traditionally the *angelus* was intoned at 6:00 A.M., noon, and 6:00 P.M. But the "one last angelus" of Crane's autumn twilight is not an act of cyclical devotion. It is a final effort: one last attempt to confer sacramental value on pain. If it fails, nothing will be able to "shield love from despair" (l. 69).

Of pain that Emily, that Isadora knew![31]   65
While high from dim elm-chancels hung with dew, [32]
That triple-noted clause of moonlight—[33]
Yes, whip-poor-will,[34] unhusks the heart of fright,
Breaks us and saves, yes, breaks the heart, yet yields
That patience that is armour and that shields
Love from despair—when love foresees the end—
Leaf after autumnal leaf
                        break off,
                                descend—
                                        descend—[35]

31. Emily Dickinson and Isadora Duncan "knew" the "stilly note of pain" in the sense both of recognizing it and of possessing the means to express it. The epigraph by Duncan identifies the pain with thwarted idealism, a reading equally consistent with the tenor of "Quaker Hill" and the lines omitted from the epigraph by Dickinson.

32. A chancel is the eastern part of a church, usually containing the choir and a high altar and separated from the rest by a screen. The chancel here is formed metaphorically by a stand of elm trees; its easterly location intimates an impending sunrise, although one that will not actually occur until the concluding poem, "Atlantis." The imagery recalls Shakespeare's Sonnet 73:

> That time of year thou mayst in me behold
> When yellow leaves, or none, or few, do hang
> Upon those boughs which shake against the cold,
> Bare ruined choirs, where late the sweet birds sang.
> In me thou see'st the twilight of such day
> As after sunset fadeth in the west;
> Which by and by black night doth take away,
> Death's second self, that seals up all in rest. (ll. 1–8)

33. The "triple-noted clause": as the next line explains, the three whistled notes sounding like *whip-poor-will* that are said to give the bird its name. The whip-poor-will in the elm-chancel enacts naturalized forms of the sacred offices, hymnody and communion, associated with the choir and altar. The bird's three notes may also suggest a naturalizing play on the Trinity.

34. Crane's whip-poor-will can claim both the songbird of Keats's "Ode to a Nightingale" and the hermit thrush of Whitman's "When Lilacs Last in the Dooryard Bloom'd" as ancestors. All three birds sing at dusk; all are invisible; and the song of each heightens the listener's awareness of mortality and at the same time consoles him for it.

35. The grammar of the typographically descending last line is significant: it is imperative, not indicative. The descent it enjoins belongs less to the season than to the poem, which is about to "descend" into the next section's nightmarish "Tunnel" as a precondition for reaching the mythographic sunrise of "Atlantis."

7. Times Square at Night, ca. 1908.

VII. THE TUNNEL

To Find the Western path
Right thro' the Gates of Wrath.

—*Blake*

THE TUNNEL: Crane originally planned to entitle this section "The Subway"; many of its symbolic details are features of a typical subway ride from midtown Manhattan to Brooklyn. The transit system in the 1920s was in several respects quite unlike today's: the train lines (two at the time, later three) were leased by the city to private operators; there were almost as many elevated lines in Manhattan as there were subways; and the train doors had to be operated manually—an inconvenience with consequences that the poem exploits.

EPIGRAPH: Blake's "Morning" provides "The Tunnel" with an implicit model:

> To find the Western path
> Right thro' the Gates of Wrath
> I urge my way.
> Sweet Mercy leads me on,
> With soft repentant moan
> I see the break of day.
>
> The War of swords and spears
> Melted by dewy tears
> Exhales on high.
> The Sun is freed from fears
> And with soft grateful tears
> Ascends the sky.

Like Blake's, Crane's text describes a journey toward dawn that begins in the west, although "The Tunnel" ends before the dawn arrives. For Crane, the journey is a descent, as the close of "Quaker Hill" has foretold; the place of "The Tunnel" in *The Bridge* is like that of the *catabasis*, the descent to the Underworld, in Homer's *Odyssey* and Virgil's *Aeneid*, whose protagonists make the journey down on their way, respectively, to finding the way home and to founding a great city. In a letter to Otto Kahn (March 18, 1926), Crane explains that his modern underworld, identified with the subway system, represents "the encroachment of machinery on humanity; a kind of purgatory in relation to the open sky."

Performances, assortments, résumés–
Up Times Square to Columbus Circle[1] lights
Channel the congresses, nightly sessions,[2]
Refractions of the thousand theatres, faces–
Mysterious kitchens. . . . You shall search them all.[3] 5
Someday by heart you'll learn each famous sight
And watch the curtain lift in hell's despite;
You'll find the garden in the third act dead,[4]

1. Times Square, at the intersection of Seventh Avenue, Broadway, and 42nd Street, was named in 1904 for the then-new building occupied by the *New York Times*; starting in 1928 the building displayed news headlines (Crane's "résumés") on a band of electric lights wrapped around its façade near the base. By 1910, Times Square had became the hub of the nation's premier theater district, housing over forty theaters with brightly illuminated marquees inside a thirteen-block radius; new theaters continued to open throughout the next decade and into the 1920s. Crane is describing the river of lights running north along Broadway—nicknamed the Great White Way as early as 1902 for its extravagant illumination—toward Columbus Circle at the southwest corner of Central Park, by 59th Street. Completed in 1905, Columbus Circle is the point from which official distances to and from New York are measured. A major traffic hub, the circle centers on a pillared statue of Columbus by Gaetano Russo, erected in 1892 as part of the city's commemoration of the four-hundredth anniversary of Columbus's first voyage. Columbus Circle thus links "The Tunnel" to "Ave Maria." It may be worth noting, in this connection, that the statue's column is decorated with reliefs of Columbus's ships; an angel holding a globe adorns the pedestal.

2. "Congresses" carries a sexual innuendo, as "nightly sessions" probably does also, while referring literally to nightly shows at theaters and clubs.

3. In the context of walking the streets at night, this line probably echoes the recurrent phrase "known them all," from T. S. Eliot's "The Love Song of J. Alfred Prufrock." Crane noted the prevalence of an "Eliot mood" on the "first page" of "The Tunnel" (to Yvor Winters, April 29, 1927).

4. The curtain that, when lifted, reveals only a dead garden recalls Shelley:

> Lift not the painted veil which those who live
> Call Life: though unreal shapes be pictured there,
> And it but mimic all we would believe . . .
> I knew one who had lifted it—he sought,
> For his lost heart was tender, things to love,
> But found them not, alas! nor was there aught
> The world contains, the which he could approve. (ll. 1–3, 7–10)

The phrase "in hell's despite" inverts "in heaven's despite" from the final stanza of Blake's "The Clod and the Pebble," spoken by the pebble in answer to the clod of clay: "Love seeketh only Self to please, / To bind another to its delight, / Joys in another's loss of ease, / And builds a hell in heaven's despite." The pebble's hell is the kingdom of desire, its heaven that of self-denial; Crane's inversion foresees a denouement in which desire fails under the pressure of modern life. The subsequent lines continue the "Eliotic mood" in keeping with this portent; their imagery echoes that of Eliot's "Preludes," e.g.:

> You dozed, and watched the night revealing
> The thousand sordid images
> Of which your soul was constituted . . .
> Sitting along the bed's edge, where
> You curled the papers from your hair,

Finger your knees–and wish yourself in bed
With tabloid crime-sheets perched in easy sight.   10

            Then let you reach your hat
            and go.[5]
            As usual, let you—also
            walking down—exclaim
            to twelve upward leaving[6]   15
            a subscription praise
            for what time slays.[7]

Or can't you quite make up your mind to ride;
A walk is better underneath the L a brisk
Ten blocks or so before?[8] But you find yourself   20
Preparing penguin flexions of the arms,—[9]

      Or clasped the yellow soles of feet
      In the palms of both soiled hands. (ll. 26–28, 35–38)

   5. Another, more definite echo of Eliot's "Prufrock"—the famous opening lines:

      Let us go then, you and I,
      When the evening is spread out against the sky
      Like a patient etherised upon a table:
      Let us go, through certain half-deserted streets,
      The muttering retreats
      Of restless nights in one-night cheap hotels.

   6. The poet starts descending the steps to a subway entrance, while twelve others move up
the stairs to exit.
   7. "What time slays" may be an allusion to the first stanza of Ralph Waldo Emerson's
poem "Brahma": "If the red slayer think he slays, / Or if the slain think he is slain, / They
know not well the subtle ways / I keep, and pass, and turn again."
   8. During the 1920s, an elevated line ran along Ninth Avenue, parallel to the Seventh
Avenue subway; both had stops at 50th Street, which is where "a brisk ten blocks or so"
roughly positions the poet between Columbus Circle to his north and Times Square (the
nearest express stop) to his south. Deciding not to walk down Ninth, he boards the Brooklyn-
bound subway at 50th and Seventh, joining the crowds headed downtown that have preceded
him at Columbus Circle, one stop further uptown, toward and beyond Times Square, the
next stop downtown. Crane may or may not have known that the Times Square subway
station opened in 1904, the year in which the *New York Times* moved to its new building in
what then became Times Square.
   9. "Preparing penguin flexions": presumably to elbow his way through the crowd in the
subway. But the motion suggests an allusion to the characteristic walk of Charlie Chaplin's
film persona, the Little Tramp, the "pirouettes" of whose "pliant cane" Crane celebrated in
his early poem "Chaplinesque." In a letter to William Wright (October 17, 1921), Crane
explained that he was "moved to put Chaplin with the poets (of today). . . . Poetry, the
human feelings, is [*sic*] so crowded out of the humdrum, rushing, mechanical scramble of
today that the man who would preserve them must duck and camouflage for dear life to keep
them or keep himself from annihilation. I have since learned that I am by no means alone in
seeing these things in the buffooneries of the tragedian, Chaplin." Crane's admiration was
heightened after he and Chaplin became acquainted, courtesy of Waldo Frank, in 1923.

As usual you will meet the scuttle yawn:[10]
The subway yawns the quickest promise home.

Be minimum, then, to swim the hiving swarms[11]
Out of the Square, the Circle burning bright—[12]   25
Avoid the glass doors gyring at your right,[13]
Where boxed alone a second, eyes take fright
—Quite unprepared rush naked back to light:
And down beside the turnstile press the coin
Into the slot.[14] The gongs already rattle.[15]   30

And so
of cities you bespeak
subways, rivered under streets
and rivers. . . . In the car   35

10. With the epithet "scuttle," the stairwell down to the subway recalls the "subway scuttle" from which the doomed bedlamite emerges in "To Brooklyn Bridge." Linking the scuffle with the "yawn" of the stairwell intimates the entryway as a kind of hell mouth ready to swallow the traveler, an image that will return before "The Tunnel" ends. But the next line deliberately retreats into banality: the subway is simply the fastest way home.

11. "Hiving swarms": both the proverbial image of the social world as a beehive (deriving primarily from Virgil's *Georgics*) and a reminiscence of Baudelaire's description of Paris in his poem "The Seven Old Men" ("Les sept vieillards"): "Fourmillante cité, cité pleine de rêves, / Où le spectre en plein jour raccroche le passant!" ("Ant-swarming city, city full of dreams, / Where ghosts in broad daylight accost the passerby!"; ll. 1–2). Baudelaire's *fourmillante*, referring to teeming ants, ironically debases the beehive image; the lines translated here appear (in French) in Eliot's note to l. 60 of *The Waste Land*, annotating a description of the crowds moving like the dead through the "Unreal city" of London.

12. The city lights between the Square and the Circle morph into the ambiguous figure of Blake's Tyger: "Tyger, tiger, burning bright, / In the forests of the night, / What immortal hand or eye / Could frame thy fearful symmetry?" ("The Tyger," ll. 1–4). The juxtaposition of "Square" and "Circle" echoes "squaring the circle," here a paraphrase of the speaker's dilemma; ancient geometers posed the problem of how to construct a square with the same area as given circle using only a compass and straightedge. The problem is impossible to solve.

13. The speaker must choose one of two "yawning" entryways, like Homer's Odysseus forced to sail by one of the devouring monsters Scylla and Charybdis in order to avoid the other and continue his voyage home. The revolving glass doors (like Charybdis's whirlpool) threaten claustrophobic panic, but in choosing to avoid them the speaker commits himself to the equally claustrophobic box of the tunnel. As it did in "Cape Hatteras," the term *gyring* echoes Yeats's "The Second Coming": "Turning and turning in the widening gyre, / The falcon cannot hear the falconer; / Things fall apart; the center cannot hold; / Mere anarchy is loosed upon the world" (ll. 1–4).

14. The coin is a nickel, recalling both "Van Winkle" and "Cutty Sark." (Almost incredibly, the fare for unlimited travel on the transit system remained five cents from 1904 to 1948.) The famous New York City subway token was not introduced until 1953, so that the then-new fifteen-cent fare could be paid with the equivalent of a single coin.

15. The gongs announce the closing of the train doors preparatory for departure; see note 34.

8. Columbus Circle, 1913.

the overtone of motion
underground, the monotone
of motion is the sound
of other faces, also underground—[16]

"Let's have a pencil Jimmy—living now   40
at Floral Park[17]

16. This section introduces a collage of words and phrases overheard on the subway, the
sound of the "other faces, also underground" that constitutes both the overtone and the
monotone of the car's motion. In a letter to Waldo Frank (August 23, 1926), Crane describes
writing "The Tunnel" as "rather ghastly, almost surgery—and, oddly almost all from the
notes and stitches I have written while swinging on the strap at late midnights going home."
The poem contains three such passages, assemblages of verbal "found objects" that do not
function allusively. The resulting jumble forms part of the poem's purgatorial, catabasis-like
character; unlike the rest of *The Bridge* and especially unlike "Atlantis," "The Tunnel" is
littered with decontextualized fragments. Even the main text is not always decipherable with
any assurance.

17. Floral Park: a town on Long Island bordering the neighborhood of Floral Park, Queens,
named for a flower business established there in the 1870s. The place name here is important;
the place is not. Crane wrote to Yvor Winters (April 29, 1927): "All the place-names mentioned in 'The Tunnel' actually do exist, and I honestly regard it as something of a miracle
that they happened to fall into the same kind of symbolical functioning as the boat-names in
'Cutty Sark.' I have never been to Floral Park nor Gravesend Manor, but you do actually

Flatbush[18]—on the fourth of July—
like a pigeon's muddy dream—potatoes
to dig in the field—travlin the town—too—
night after night—the Culver line[19]—the   45
girls all shaping up—it used to be—"

Our tongues recant like beaten weather vanes.
This answer lives like verdigris, like hair
Beyond extinction, surcease of the bone;
And repetition freezes—"What   50

"what do you want? getting weak on the links?
fandaddle daddy don't ask for change— IS THIS
FOURTEENTH? it's half past six she said—if
you don't like my gate why did you
swing on it, why *didja*   55
swing on it
anyhow—"[20]

    And somehow anyhow swing–

The phonographs of hades in the brain
Are tunnels that re-wind themselves[21] and love60
A burnt match skating in a urinal,—[22]

take the 7th Avenue Interborough to get there, and you do change at Chambers Street." For
Interborough see n. 25; for Gravesend and Chambers Street see n. 30.
 18. Flatbush: a neighborhood in south central Brooklyn populated during the 1920s primarily by working-class Italian, Irish, and Jewish families. Flatbush experienced a surge in
population and development during the decade as a result of the expansion of subway service.
 19. The elevated Culver Line originally ran between Coney Island and Prospect Park,
Brooklyn; by 1920 it had been extended to meet the Brighton Line at West 8th Street in
Manhattan.
 20. The swinging gate carries a sexual innuendo developed in the succeeding lines. The
isolated "And somehow anyhow swing" is a contrapuntal interjection looking beyond the
tunnel to the concluding line of *The Bridge*, "Whispers antiphonal in azure swing."
 21. The compound metaphor in these lines extends the equivalence of the subway with
the underworld ("hades in the brain") to include the cacophony of lamenting souls. The
noise comes partly from the babble of overheard voices (the quoted fragments that follow
involve anger and regret) and partly from the sound of the train wheels on the tracks of the
tunnels, which become equivalent to the grooves of a phonograph record. The screech of the
wheels will return below. The "tunnels that re-wind themselves" also suggest the Cretan
labyrinth, the maze to which, according to classical mythology, the ancient Athenians annu-
ally sent youths and maidens to be sacrificed to the monster, the Minotaur, who lived there.
 22. The burnt match and the urinal recall the use of public men's rooms as sexual cruising
grounds.

Somewhere above Fourteenth TAKE THE EXPRESS
To brush some new presentiment of pain—

"But I want service in this office SERVICE
I said—after   65
the show she cried a little afterwards but—"[23]

Whose head is swinging from the swollen strap?[24]
Whose body smokes along the bitten rails,
Bursts from a smoldering bundle far behind
In back forks of the chasms of the brain,—   70
Puffs from a riven stump far out behind
In interborough fissures of the mind . . .?[25]

And why do I often meet your visage here,
Your eyes like agate lanterns[26]—on and on
Below the toothpaste and the dandruff ads?   75
—And did their riding eyes right through your side,
And did their eyes like unwashed platters ride?
And Death, aloft,—gigantically down

23. The overhead words and phrases printed in capital letters here recall the pub scene from "A Game of Chess," part 2 of Eliot's *The Waste Land*. Eliot's part 3, "The Fire Sermon," culminates with brief overhead narratives of seduction and regret similar to the one that here rounds off the last of Crane's "found passages." Like "Ave Maria," "The Tunnel" will conclude with an allusion to "The Fire Sermon."

24. The details of this stanza suggest a lynching, but not the racial hate crime appallingly common during the era. As the next segment announces, the imaginary victim is Edgar Allen Poe, personifying the American poet as an alcoholic visionary—rather like Hart Crane. (The affinity prompts the statement that Death constantly probes toward Crane through Poe.) Crane wrote to Yvor Winters (October 5, 1926) that "One goes back to Poe, and to Whitman—and always to my beloved Melville—with a renewed appreciation of what America really is, or could be." Poe lived in New York from 1842 to 1847. The image of his decapitation may be meant to recall the death of Orpheus, who was torn apart by Bacchantes enraged, according to Ovid, at any rate, by his choice of young men as lovers after the death of his wife Eurydice. Orpheus's head was cast into the Hebrus, a river in Thrace. The piercing of Poe's side by a blind or corrupted gaze (the "riding eyes" that "ride" right through like unwashed platters) connects the lynching to the crucifixion, an act of those who know not what they do.

25. "Interborough": situated between the municipal divisions (the five boroughs) of New York City. The word specifically designates the subway line on which the poet is riding toward Brooklyn, "Interborough Rapid Transit" (the IRT), one of the two privately operated lines of the day. The same train is still running today as the No. 1 Broadway local.

26. The "agate lanterns" may echo Poe's poem "To Helen," whose idolized namesake (a statue, not a woman) stands with an "agate lamp" in her hands to guide the "weary, wayworn wanderer . . . / To his own native shore."

Probing through you—toward me, O evermore![27]
And when they dragged your retching flesh,   80
Your trembling hands that night through Baltimore—[28]
That last night on the ballot rounds, did you,
Shaking, did you deny the ticket, Poe? [29]

For Gravesend Manor change at Chambers Street.[30]
The platform hurries along to a dead stop.   85

The intent escalator[31] lifts a serenade[32]
Stilly
Of shoes, umbrellas, each eye attending its shoe, then
Bolting outright somewhere above where streets
Burst suddenly in rain.[33] . . . The gongs recur.[34]   90

27. "O evermore" reverses the "nevermore" in the refrain of Poe's most famous poem, "The Raven": "Quoth the raven, 'Nevermore.'"

28. Poe was found unconscious in or near a tavern, also used as a polling place, in Baltimore on Election Day 1849; he was taken to a hospital, lapsed in and out of consciousness without being able to give a coherent account of his condition, and died a few days later, on October 7. The cause of his death is unknown.

29. A widely circulated theory of Poe's death regards him as a victim of "cooping," a form of kidnapping in which a political gang would hold someone captive in a room, or "coop," alternately beat the victim and force liquor on him, and send him out to vote repeatedly for their candidate, often with changes of clothing between votes. (The clothes Poe was found in were not his own.) Crane speculates that Poe might have been beaten to death for "denying the ticket," that is, refusing at some point to continue the charade.

30. The change at Chambers Street is from a local train to an express that will travel under the river to Brooklyn. Crane's boast (n. 17) notwithstanding, "Gravesend Manor" is not a real place name, though "Gravesend" is. The neighborhood of Gravesend, one of the earliest villages in Brooklyn, borders Coney Island; the transit lines that service it include the elevated Culver Line, which Crane mentions above. A resort area in the nineteenth century, in Crane's day Gravesend was in decline; its mention here probably has more to do with its name than with its history.

31. The train has gone one stop beyond Chambers Street to Park Place, a deep station where an escalator had been installed in 1919; the poet observes or imagines the passengers exiting and rising toward the street while he remains on the train.

32. A serenade is literally music meant to be performed at evening, traditionally by a lover in the street to his lady above, at a window or on a balcony. Here the rising music becomes the mechanical rumble of the 1920s escalator; the romantic encounter becomes the isolation of strangers in the crowd.

33. The passengers rising on the escalator may be awaiting deliverance from their purgatorial journey through the underworld; the sudden rain into which the poet imagines them bolting recapitulates the cloudburst wished for in *The Waste Land* as a source of rebirth and redemption. But another facet of the "Eliot mood" qualifies the prospect in advance; the rising passengers' downcast eyes recall Eliot's "each man fixed his eyes before his feet / Flowed up the hill and down King William Street" (from "The Burial of the Dead," part 1 of *The Waste Land*)—the image, derived from Dante, of the modern city as a limbo filled with crowds of the walking dead.

34. Unlike the evocative "gongs in white surplices" of "The Harbor Dawn," the gongs in "The Tunnel" are obtrusive. In Crane's day, subway dispatchers sounded a gong to instruct

Elbows and levers, guard and hissing door.[35]
Thunder is galvothermic here below. . . . The car
Wheels off. The train rounds, bending to a scream,
Taking the final level for the dive
Under the river—[36]   95
And somewhat emptier than before,
Demented, for a hitching second, humps; then
Lets go. . . . Toward corners of the floor
Newspapers wing, revolve and wing.[37]
Blank windows gargle signals through the roar.   100

And does the Daemon take you home, also,[38]
Wop washerwoman, with the bandaged hair?[39]
After the corridors are swept, the cuspidors—
The gaunt sky-barracks cleanly now, and bare,[40]

the guards (see the next note) to close the train doors after a forty-five-second stop in the station.

35. The New York subways formerly employed guards to control passenger movement on and off the trains and, during the 1920s before the introduction of automatic controls, to open and close the car doors. The guards' job was to move people quickly, which they did by both shouting and shoving. Their call of "Step lively!" was infamous, and they were widely reviled as brutal "pushers-in" and "sardine-packers."

36. The subway tracks curve at this point, as the line heads eastward under the river; the result is a loud squeal as the train takes the curve. The image forms a chthonic parallel (part travesty, part anticipation) of the soaring "curveship" of the Bridge that stands as the journey's end.

37. The newspapers discarded on the floor of the subway car, perhaps suggesting the tabloid crime sheets mentioned earlier, "revolve and wing" like the gull whose "dip and pivot" over New York harbor opens *The Bridge*. The reminiscent image is once again part travesty, part prophecy; the ambiguity is consistent with the poem's purgatorial genre.

38. Daemons in classical mythology are supernatural beings intermediate between gods and humans. In Plato's *Symposium* they are described as intermediaries who transport "to the gods the prayers and sacrifices of men, and to men the commands and rewards of the gods." Later accounts incorporate the elements of possession and malevolence familiar from the Christian cognate, *demon*. Crane blends the two conceptions; his Daemon, literally the subway train, is an impromptu monster whose "eventful and demurring yawn" (six lines below, echoing the earlier yawn of the staircase) devours and then regurgitates the travelers.

39. The ethnic slur joins the winged newspapers and screaming curve as a mixed purgatorial image. The washerwoman is an avatar of Columbus, to whom she is linked through her Genoese origin, and also of Pocahontas, with whom she shares the sheaf of hair (three lines below) associated in "The Dance" with flowing water and the "warm sibilance" of the wind over grass. Initially the washerwoman's hair is "bandaged," that is, covered with a kerchief or bandana used as a sweatband at work, but Crane imagines her letting her "golden hair" down (like the Mary/Rapunzel of "Virginia") with her "mother eyes and hand" when she reaches home. "Golden hair" may also suggest the portrait of a Renaissance lady superimposed on the figure of the working-class immigrant.

40. The "gaunt sky-barracks" is one of the city's skyscrapers, the office building cleaned after business hours by the washerwoman, who, like the poet, heads home late at night.

O Genoese, do you bring mother eyes and hands,   105
Back home to children and to golden hair?

Daemon, demurring and eventful yawn![41]
Whose hideous laughter is a bellows mirth
—Or the muffled slaughter of a day in birth—
O cruelly to inoculate the brinking dawn   110
With antennae toward worlds that glow and sink;—
To spoon us out more liquid than the dim
Locution of the eldest star, and pack
The conscience navelled in the plunging wind,
Umbilical to call—and straightway die![42]   115

O caught like pennies beneath soot and steam,
Kiss of our agony thou gatherest;[43]
Condensed, thou takest all—shrill ganglia
Impassioned with some song we fail to keep.

41. In addition to reiterating the traditional image of the devouring mouth of hell, the
yawning Daemon may allude to the demurring monster Ennui, who would "swallow up the
world in a yawn" in "Au lecteur" ("To the Reader"), the first poem of Baudelaire's *Flowers
of Evil.*

42. The basic conceit of this difficult segment is that the Daemon mocks and stifles the
coming of dawn; it would "slaughter," that is, abort, the "day in birth" in an allegorical
replay of the biblical slaughter of the innocents (Matthew 2:16). The tunnel's noisy windings
act as broadcast antennae (compare the "radio static./The captured fume of space foam," in
"Cape Hatteras," ll. 18–19), whose signal cruelly "inoculates" the dawn "toward"— that is,
in resistance to—the cosmic harmony represented throughout *The Bridge* by the alternation
of the Evening and Morning stars, "worlds that glow and sink." The "plunging wind" of the
Daemon's "bellows laugh" feeds the fire of a forge that melts our identity down and spoons
us out onto the street; the image exacerbates Eliot's "I have measured out my life with coffee
spoons" from "The Love Song of J. Alfred Prufrock" (l. 51). The "dim locution of the eldest
star" remains obscure; perhaps Crane knew that the supposed "influence" of the stars on
human life was once thought of as a rarefied fluid; perhaps he was thinking of the "great star"
that falls from the heavens in Revelation 8:11: "And the name of the star is called Wormwood:
and the third part of the waters became wormwood; and many men died of the waters,
because they were made bitter." Finally, the Daemon destroys conscience by rendering it
unborn: packing it (the word plays on the subway guards' "packing" of the riders) into the
form of a navel joined to the umbilicus of the plunging wind winding through the tunnel.
Crane's phrase "Umbilical to call" may allude to a passage in the "Proteus" section of James
Joyce's *Ulysses* in which Stephen Dedalus, after observing a "misbirth with a trailing navel-
cord," imagines the umbilicus as a telephone line stretching back through history: "Hello.
. . . Put me on to Edenville. Aleph, alpha: nought, nought one."

43. The "kiss of our agony," suggesting the kiss by which Judas betrayed Jesus, is gathered
by the tunnel just as pennies dropped through grates on the street are gathered by the transit
system's ventilation shafts. The network of tunnels forms a shrill external nervous system
that appropriates "the songs we fail to keep" under the stress of mechanized modern life; the
sound of our loss becomes audible in the screech of the trains as heard faintly through the
grates underfoot.

And yet, like Lazarus, to feel the slope,   120
The sod and billow breaking,—lifting ground,[44]
—A sound of waters bending astride the sky[45]
Unceasing with some Word that will not die . . .!

* * *

A tugboat, wheezing wreaths of steam,
Lunged past, with one galvanic blare stove up the River.[46] 125
I counted the echoes assembling, one after one,
Searching, thumbing the midnight on the piers.
Lights, coasting, left the oily tympanum of waters;
The blackness somewhere gouged glass on a sky.[47]
And this thy harbor, O my city, I have driven under,   130
Tossed from the coil of ticking towers.[48] . . . Tomorrow,
And to be.[49] . . . Here by the River that is East[50]—

44. Lazarus, four days dead, is resurrected by Jesus in John 11:38–53; the poet feels like the awakening Lazarus as the train, having crossed under the river, ascends toward his destination on the Brooklyn side.

45. The bending waters suggest a rainbow, perhaps identical to the arc of the bridge; that the sense involved is hearing rather than sight recalls the image of the Bridge as a harp from "To Brooklyn Bridge" and anticipates its elaboration in "Atlantis." The covenantal association of the rainbow is consistent with the invocation of the Logos in the next line, also embodied in the Bridge—"one arc synoptic of all tides below," as "Atlantis" will call it.

46. The sound and motion of the tugboat transmute the "Far strum of foghorns . . . signals dispersed in veils" of "The Harbor Dawn"; the change is from the evocative to the grotesque, but the moment nonetheless forms a "wheeze" and "lunge" of release from passage through the tunnel. Its echoes, which the next two lines show the poet counting and trying to "read" as he starts "thumbing through the midnight," segue into the poem's visionary conclusion.

47. The lights on the tug recede as the boat passes upriver, leaving the poet alone with the dark waters, the now silent tympanum (drumhead or membrane of the inner ear) from which the tug's blare had resounded. (The phrase "oily tympanum" may echo Eliot's "The river sweats / Oil and tar" and "beating oars" from "The Fire Sermon.") The resulting blackness, like a defaced nether sky, corresponds to the experience of kenosis, the emptying out of self or dark night of the soul, through which the poet must pass before his gaze can find the Bridge.

48. The towers are the skyscrapers of Manhattan, "ticking" because they are governed by the clock time that also governs the movement of those who work in the buildings and who travel to and fro on the subway. "Coil" echoes the proverbial "mortal coil," originally from Shakespeare's *Hamlet*. It also picks up the metaphor of the tunnel as an umbilical cord in lines 113–14; emergence from the subway corresponds to rebirth as the poet leaves the subway with the Brooklyn Bridge in sight.

49. "Tomorrow, / And to be": fragmentary echoes reversing the despair of Shakespeare's Macbeth ("Tomorrow, and tomorrow, and tomorrow, / Creeps in this petty pace from day to day") and Hamlet ("To be or not to be, that is the question").

50. Leaving Manhattan, "my city," behind, the poet has crossed the East River—symbolically, the river of dawn, "the river that is East"—into Brooklyn, where he can catch sight of Atlantis along the arc of the Bridge. His arrival completes both a symbolic complement to Columbus's voyage of discovery from east to west and the journey announced in Blake's "Morning" from west (the West Side of Manhattan) to east, corresponding to the passage from night to the first hours of the morning.

Here at the waters' edge the hands drop memory;[51]
Shadowless in that abyss they unaccounting lie.
How far away the star has pooled the sea—[52]   135
Or shall the hands be drawn away, to die?

Kiss of our agony Thou gatherest,
                    O Hand of Fire
                              gatherest—[53]

51. The "dropping" of memory suggests that the East River merges at morning with Lethe, the river of forgetfulness in the classical underworld; in Virgil's *Aeneid*, souls destined for reincarnation drink from Lethe to forget their former lives. The hands in Crane's text release the burden of memory and extend, palms open, into the "abyss" of the future (compare "tomorrow / And to be" in the preceding lines), a pure potentiality (they are "shadowless" there) that they cannot yet account for.

52. The morning star turns the sea into a mirror, though only in the distance; the line complements the paradisal reflection of the evening star in "Cape Hatteras": "Adam and Adam's answer in the forest / Left Hesperus mirrored in the lucid pool" (ll. 30–31).

53. The Hand of Fire, the divine hand recalled from "Ave Maria," now gathers the "kiss of our agony" in a redemptive sense and transmutes the "bellows mirth" of the Daemon's "hideous laughter" into the poet's ecstatic outcry. As in "Ave Maria," the image of the hand plays on the conclusion to Eliot's "The Fire Sermon":

To Carthage then I came

Burning burning burning burning
O Lord Thou pluckest me out
O Lord Thou pluckest

burning (ll. 307–11)

Eliot's notes refer most of this passage to the *Confessions* of St. Augustine and quote the source of l. 307: "To Carthage then I came, where a cauldron of unholy loves sang all about mine ears"; the note to l. 309 reads, in part, "From St. Augustine's *Confessions* again." The reiterated "burning" echoes the Buddha's "Fire Sermon," which describes the senses as burning with passion, aversion, delusion, and suffering.

9. The Bound Cable Strands," 1915.

VIII. ATLANTIS

Music is then the knowledge of that which relates to love
in harmony and system.

—*Plato*

ATLANTIS: The first section of *The Bridge* to be written, "Atlantis" is actually the source of the many images it serves to recapitulate. "It is symphonic," Crane wrote, "in including the convergence of all the strands separately detailed in antecedent sections of the poem—Columbus, conquests of water, land, etc. Pokahantus [*sic*] , subways, offices, etc. . . . The Bridge in becoming a ship, a world, a woman, a tremendous harp (as it does finally) seems to really have a career. I have attempted to induce the same feelings of elation, etc—like being carried forward and upward simultaneously—. . . that one experiences in walking across my beloved Brooklyn Bridge" (to Waldo Frank, January 18, 1926). The myth of Atlantis derives from Plato, whose *Timaeus* refers to a vast island, the former center of a far-flung empire, already ancient and long since sunken under the sea. In *Critias*, Plato describes the Atlanteans as builders of great canals, tunnels, towers, and, of course, bridges.

EPIGRAPH: From Plato's *Symposium*, as translated by Shelley ("The Banquet of Plato"). Crane's design for "Atlantis" may also draw on Plato's description of the harmony of the spheres in book 10 of *The Republic*: "The spindle [of the cosmos] turns on the knees of Necessity; and on the upper surface of each circle is a siren, who goes round with them, hymning a single tone or note. The eight together form one harmony." Crane simulates this "harmony and system" by composing "Atlantis" in eight-line stanzas whose "numbers" (in the traditional sense of "verses") correspond to the notes of the octave in the diatonic scale. Recurrent though irregular rhyme renders the stanzas "musical" and the rotation of the stanzas—there are twelve of them, one, perhaps, for each pitch in the chromatic scale—render the poem's harmony and system "symphonic."

Through the bound cable strands, the arching path
Upward, veering with light, the flight of strings,[1]—
Taut miles of shuttling moonlight syncopate
The whispered rush, telepathy of wires.
Up the index of night, granite and steel—
Transparent meshes—fleckless the gleaming staves—
Sibylline voices flicker, waveringly stream
As though a god were issue of the strings. . . .

And through that cordage, threading with its call   9
One arc synoptic of all tides below—[2]
Their labyrinthine mouths of history[3]
Pouring reply as though all ships at sea
Complighted in one vibrant breath made cry,—

---

1. . This stanza is best annotated as a whole. Like "To Brooklyn Bridge," "Atlantis" metaphorically identifies the Bridge with an Aeolian harp (see "Southern Cross," n. 8) and with the lyre of Apollo, inverted in the last line so that the god, not his song, is the issue (outcome, offspring, outpouring) of the strings (the bound cable strands). The double metaphor is doubly compounded: by the image of weaving (the shuttling moonlight is drawn in horizontal lines across the vertical cables, adding shifted accents—syncopations—to the whispered rush of the wind through the strands) and by the image of the Bridge as a musical score (the cables as gleaming staves, the collection of lines and spaces on which music is notated; "staves" also refers to the stanzas of a poem). In both cases, sound and light fuse synesthetically: the moonlight sounds in the wind and the gleaming cable-staves are filled with light rather than with written notes (hence, the staves are "fleckless"). Similarly, the Sibylline voices of the Bridge, perhaps recalling the singing of Plato's Sirens, appear as flickering light, not as sound. "Sibylline" means oracular or prophetic; in classical mythology a sibyl was a woman of great age who prophesied in verse while in an ecstatic trance. Crane may have meant the allusion as a riposte to the epigraph of Eliot's *The Waste Land*, where the Sibyl of Apollo at Cumae, ravaged by extreme old age, says she wants to die.

2. "Cordage" refers simultaneously to any assembly of strings, lines, ropes, cables, and the like; to the braiding together of strands to form rope or, in this case, the steel cables joined to the granite of the bridge towers; and to the rigging of a ship. The term fuses the Bridge as harp and lyre with the Bridge as sailing ship (recalling both "Ave Maria" and "Cutty Sark"); the arc of the Bridge acts as a synopsis of the globe-circling movement of all ships at sea and of its cosmic counterpart, the music of the spheres. The "call" of the cordage is the music of the "gleaming staves" that uphold the Bridge materially and describe it poetically.

3. "Their labyrinthine mouths of history" are those of the seven oceans mentioned at the end of the stanza; they answer the sibylline voices of prophecy by "pouring reply" with a "vibrant breath" that further animates the cordage of the bridge. Their cry voices a communal pledge, as Crane suggests with the neologism "complighted," suggesting a general plighting of trust or troth.

"Make thy love sure—to weave whose song we ply!"[4]
—From black embankments, moveless soundings hailed,
So seven oceans answer from their dream.[5]

And on, obliquely up bright carrier bars   17
New octaves trestle the twin monoliths[6]
Beyond whose frosted capes[7] the moon bequeaths
Two worlds of sleep (O arching strands of song!)—
Onward and up the crystal-flooded aisle[8]
White tempest nets file upward, upward ring
With silver terraces the humming spars,[9]
The loft of vision, palladium helm of stars[10]

---

4. The ships trace and retrace—"ply"—their routes and in so doing weave together ("ply") the song of the love that is to be made "sure" by the weaving of the Bridge (and *The Bridge*) as "our Myth" ("Cape Hatteras": "our Myth, whereof I sing!"; l. 191). Taken together with the "threading" of the Bridge's cordage and the injunction to make love sure, this plying may recall the late phases of voyaging in Homer's *Odyssey*. As Odysseus continues to ply his oars homeward, his wife Penelope publicly vows not to marry again until she has finished work on a funeral shroud that, still hoping for her husband's return, she weaves by day and unweaves by night.

5. The seven oceans are the proverbial "seven seas"—not specific bodies of water but the waters of the world taken as a whole. To have sailed the seven seas is to have sailed around the globe.

6. The twin monoliths are the support towers that give the Bridge its footing in the riverbed; between these run the horizontal cables, the "carrier bars," from which more delicate, harp-like vertical cable strands are suspended, forming a trestle of "new octaves" in the sense both of new musical scales and new verses.

7. "Frosted" by moonlight, the monoliths jut upward like promontories, recalling "Cape Hatteras" and answering the question posed in Whitman's "Passage to India": "Propulsion to what capes?"

8. The aisle is the walkway of the Bridge, "crystal-flooded" because its ascent seems to lead the observer into the upper reaches of the cosmos, whose musical spheres, in traditional Pythagorean cosmology, were composed of crystal.

9. The "white tempest nets" are the moonlit cable strands visualized as sails, in keeping with the metaphor of the Bridge as a sailing ship. The metaphor continues in the "silver terraces," suggesting ranks of bright sails billowed by the wind, which "ring" the ship's spars—its masts and booms—in two senses: surrounding them and making them ring and hum in sympathetic vibration with the cosmic harmony. The bridge-ship aspires to the "loft of vision," both the high point of its arc and the highest circle of the heavens, the sphere of the fixed stars.

10. In classical civilization, a palladium was an image of great antiquity thought to offer protection to the city that possessed it. The most famous palladium was a wooden statue of Athena in the citadel of Troy; according to Virgil's *Aeneid*, it was stolen by Odysseus and Diomedes and later carried by Aeneas to the site of the future Rome. Crane identifies the helmet ("helm") of Athena with the band of stars in the highest celestial sphere as glimpsed from the Bridge, which (like the Statue of Liberty in "To Brooklyn Bridge") extends the protection of the palladium to the modern city.

Sheerly the eyes, like seagulls stung with rime—[11]   25
Slit and propelled by glistening fins of light—[12]
Pick biting way up towering looms that press
Sidelong with flight of blade on tendon blade
—Tomorrows into yesteryear—and link
What cipher-script of time no traveler reads
But who, through smoking pyres of love and death,
Searches the timeless laugh of mythic spears.

Like hails, farewells—up planet-sequined heights   33
Some trillion whispering hammers glimmer Tyre:[13]
Serenely, sharply up the long anvil cry
Of inchling aeons silence rivets Troy.[14]

---

11. "Rime" probably puns on "rhyme," but the essential point in this and the following line is that the observer's eyes are dazzled ("stung" to the point of tears) by the glittering spectacle of the Bridge merged with the night sky. The stanza, like the first, is best glossed as a whole; its sense, however, is probably less important than its array of multiply compounded metaphors recapitulating motifs from antecedent sections of *The Bridge*: the seagull of "To Brooklyn Bridge," the towers of "Three Songs," the planes ("flight of blade on tendon blade") of "Cape Hatteras," and the sacrificial pyre of "The Dance." As eyes travel upward, the observer understands that the Bridge links the future with the past ("Tomorrows into yesteryear") by forming a kind of mystic writing, the "cipher-script of time" (an image resonant with the "index of night" in stanza 1). The writing is also a kind of weaving formed by the linked cables strung on the "looms" of the bridge. This script can be deciphered only by one who searches for what is timeless amid the passions of time (the "pyres of love and death"). "What cipher-script of time no traveler reads" may carry a light echo of Hamlet's "The undiscovered country from whose bourne / No traveler returns." The "timeless laugh of mystic spears" is implacably obscure, but it may be reminiscent of Blake's "The Tyger," in which the tiger's "fearful symmetry" derives from its creator's work with hammer and anvil at a divine forge and prompts the speaker to exclaim: "When the stars threw down their spears, / And watered heaven with their tears, / Did he smile his work to see?" (ll. 17–19). The hammer and anvil show up in Crane's next stanza.

12. The "fins of light" are the electric arc lamps illuminating the Bridge (as they had done since its opening); throughout "Atlantis," the bridge lights tend to merge with the light of the stars.

13. In another fusion of light and sound, the musical cordage of the Bridge against the sky makes the ancient Phoenician city of Tyre appear in glimmers. Tyre is the first in a sequence of images drawn from fallen civilizations and failed voyages redeemed by the Bridge. A port city in present-day Lebanon, Tyre was the center of maritime commerce in the ancient world; Tyrian merchants were the first Mediterranean navigators. The city was built on an island, but after Alexander the Great conquered it in 322 BCE, he connected Tyre to the mainland by building a causeway—that is, a kind of bridge. Sediment from shifting ocean currents subsequently made the causeway into an isthmus. Numerous Old Testament prophecies foretell the destruction of Tyre.

14. Another, more famous lost city makes its appearance next: Troy, whose palladium the third stanza has already appropriated. The Bridge consummates the long history of metalwork, whose "anvil cry" is sublimated into light and silence (a pause in the prevailing music) along the series of suspension cables. The cable strands compress aeons to inchlings; the points of light become the rivets that rebuild Troy as a vision of Atlantis.

And you, aloft there—Jason! [15] Hesting Shout![16]
Still wrapping harness to the swarming air!
Silvery the rushing wake, surpassing call,
Beams yelling Aeolus! splintered in the straits![17]

From gulfs unfolding, terrible of drums,   41
Tall Vision-of-the-Voyage,[18] tensely spare—
Bridge, lifting night to cycloramic crest
Of deepest day[19]—O choir, translating time
Into what multitudinous Verb the suns
And synergy of waters ever fuse, recast
In myriad syllables,[20]—Psalm of Cathay![21]
O Love, thy white, pervasive Paradigm . . .!

15. Further aloft, as if atop a mast where he harnesses the air, appears the mythical figure
of Jason, a classical precursor of Columbus. Leading a band of heroes known as the Argonauts
after their ship, the *Argo*, Jason set forth on an epic voyage in search of the Golden Fleece.
Crane's choice of Jason as a quest hero may echo Shelley's poem "Hellas," which also incor-
porates another motif important to *The Bridge*:

> The world's great age begins anew,
> The golden years return,
> The earth doth like a snake renew
> Her wintry weeds outworn. . . .

> A loftier Argo claims the main,
> Fraught with a later prize;
> Another Orpheus sings again,
> And loves, and weeps, and dies. (ll. 1–4, 13–16)

16. "Hesting": commanding.

17. Aeolus, the god of the winds, was Jason's great-grandfather. Crane seems to fuse
Jason's death with the shipwrecks and plane crashes evoked in "Cape Hatteras"; revisiting
the *Argo* after the ship had been abandoned, Jason was killed by a falling beam.

18. The address to the Bridge as "Vision-of-the-Voyage" is simultaneously a description,
an interpretation, and a christening; the epithet momentarily transforms the Bridge into one
of the clipper ships in the "phantom regatta" observed from its heights in "Cutty Sark."

19. A cyclorama is a panoramic painting, usually of a historic event or famous place, lining
the interior walls of a circular platform; a spectator positioned at the center of the platform
has a 360-degree view of the image. Cycloramas were a popular form of entertainment in
nineteenth-century cities; their spectacles often featured musical accompaniment. Crane's
metaphor takes the zenith of the Bridge's arc as the center of a cyclorama of dawn, merging
the resumption of the dawn theme initiated in "The Tunnel" with the first direct address to
the Bridge in "Atlantis."

20. The Bridge, now a choir of voices, translates (historical) time into the complex verb *to
bridge*: even the noun *bridge* is verblike because the action of a bridge in bridging is perpetual.
The suns and synergies of waters fuse the multitudinous agencies of this verb into a single
form and recast it in "myriad syllables"; the latter belong both to the material "cipher-script"
of stanza 2 and to the words of the poem.

21. "Psalm of Cathay" recalls the aim of Columbus's voyage of discovery from "Ave
Maria" and echoes Jason's quest for the Golden Fleece. The Bridge as Psalm elevates Cathay
from a secular dream to a sacred metaphor.

We left the haven hanging in the night— 49
Sheened harbor lanterns backward fled the keel.[22]
Pacific here at time's end, bearing corn,—
Eyes stammer through the pangs of dust and steel.
And still the circular, indubitable frieze
Of heaven's meditation, yoking wave
To kneeling wave, one song devoutly binds—[23]
The vernal strophe chimes from deathless strings!

O Thou steeled Cognizance whose leap commits 57
The agile precincts of the lark's return;[24]
Within whose lariat sweep encinctured sing
In single chrysalis the many twain,[25]—
Of stars Thou art the stitch and stallion glow[26]

22. Another stanza best glossed as a whole. The first two lines describe a ship departing from an illuminated haven or harbor, whose lights recede (flee the keel, seem to move backward) as the ship departs. The voyage and the voyagers remain obscure, but their course seems to pass through the darkness and toward the luminous Bridge, which arches in the second half of the stanza in its multiple identities of harp, choir, curve of "heaven's meditation" and—a new addition—frieze. The voyage seems as much temporal as spatial; the voyagers reach "time's end"—not its conclusion but its goal—where they, or it, become "pacific" as they, or it, bear corn, recalling the association of Pocahontas and the natural cycle in "The Dance." The voyagers have reached this end despite the pangs of modern life, symbolized by dust and steel; their "stammering" eyes find relief in the Bridge, so that what the eyes see, their "vision" in the grand sense, becomes doubly articulate: in the "vernal strophe" of the Bridge's devout song and its counterpart in the verses of the poem.

23. "One song devoutly binds": compare Matthew 16:19, quoting Jesus: "And I will give unto thee the keys of the kingdom of heaven; and whatsoever thou shalt bind on earth shall be bound in heaven; and whatsoever thou shalt loose on earth shall be loosed in heaven."

24. The curving leap of the Bridge both ascends toward heaven and returns to earth with divine knowledge, thus forming a "steeled Cognizance." "Steeled" means both "firm" and "made of steel." The circular journey "commits," that is, enacts and commits itself to, the lark's return by completing the trajectory of both Shelley's skylark, "That from Heaven, or near it, / Pourest [its] full heart / In profuse strains of unpremeditated art" ("To a Sky-Lark," ll. 3–5) and Shakespeare's, "the lark [that] at break of day arising / From sullen earth, sings hymns at heaven's gate" (Sonnet 39, ll. 11–12). The European skylark sings only in flight, usually when too far aloft to be seen.

25. The "many twain" most prominently include time and space, history and myth, together with the various avatars of these pairings that recur throughout *The Bridge*. The chrysalis is a traditional symbol of metamorphosis; in Greek the word for the butterfly that takes wing from the chrysalis is *psyche*, which also means soul.

26. The "stallion glow" of the stars picks up the image of the Bridge's curve as the sweep of a lariat (l. 59); the horse thus roped in is presumably the constellation Pegasus, representing the white winged horse of Greek mythology. Pegasus symbolizes the flight of poetry, because the beat of his hoof on the earth brought forth the Hippocrene, the spring of the Muses on Mount Helicon. The Bridge as the "stitch" connecting the stars may recall Whitman's "Song of Myself": "Through me many long dumb voices. . . . / Voices of cycles of preparation and accretion, / And of the threads that connect the stars, and of wombs and of the father-stuff" (24.509, 511–12).

And like an organ, Thou, with sound of doom—
Sight, sound and flesh Thou leadest from time's realm
As love strikes clear direction for the helm.

Swift peal of secular light, intrinsic Myth[27]   65
Whose fell unshadow is death's utter wound,—[28]
O River-throated—iridescently upborne
Through the bright drench and fabric of our veins;
With white escarpments swinging into light,[29]
Sustained in tears the cities are endowed
And justified conclament with ripe fields[30]
Revolving through their harvests in sweet torment.

Forever Deity's glittering Pledge, O Thou   73
Whose canticle fresh chemistry assigns
To wrapt inception and beatitude,—[31]
Always through blinding cables, to our joy,
Of thy white seizure springs the prophecy:
Always through spiring cordage,[32] pyramids

27. The Bridge is "intrinsic Myth" because, as noted at the end of "To Brooklyn Bridge,"
it is not a mythical symbol but the myth itself in material form.

28. The Bridge casts an "unshadow" because it illuminates the night. As "Death's utter
wound," that is, the fatal wound dealt to, not by, Death, the Bridge in Crane's coinage
reverses the traditional image of "the valley of the shadow of death" (Psalm 23) and recalls I
Corinthians 15:54–55: "Then shall be brought to pass the saying that is written, Death is
swallowed up in victory. O Death, where is thy sting?" The death of Death may also recall
the last line of John Donne's Holy Sonnet 10: "And Death shall be no more; Death, thou
shalt die!"

29. The white escarpments of the Bridge are the lines of its lights in the shape of steep
slopes. The image fuses or reconciles modern technology with the forms of nature, a project
that continues throughout the remainder of the stanza.

30. "Conclament" is Crane's misspelling of *conclamant*, "calling out together." The Bridge
renders the landscape of urban modernity the equal and counterpart of the pastoral image of
a fertile continent attuned to the cycle of nature. The image of the ripened harvest redeems
the broken autumn of "Quaker Hill" and may draw indirectly on the patriotic images of
"amber waves of grain" and "the fruited plain" in the song "America, the Beautiful" (composed 1910).

31. "Wrapt" is Crane's spelling for "rapt." The "fresh chemistry" by which the Bridge
transfigures the rapt spectator is probably a nonce usage designating alchemy, whose dream
of transmuting base metals into gold was understood in its day as a spiritual allegory or
discipline aimed at wisdom and immortality. A canticle may be any hymn with a biblical text
other than a psalm, but Crane's usage probably carries a pair of more specific allusions: to the
celebration of love in the Song of Solomon (familiarly known as the Song of Songs or Canticle
of Canticles) and to the liturgical singing of canticles after morning and evening prayer.

32. The cordage is "spiring" in the ascending form celebrated by Crane; the term suggests
the shape of a church spire and plays phonetically on the cognate *aspiring*.

Of silver sequel,[33] Deity's young name
Kinetic of white choiring wings[34] . . . ascends.

Migrations that must needs void memory,
Inventions that cobblestone the heart,—
Unspeakable Thou Bridge to Thee, O Love.
Thy pardon for this history, whitest Flower,
O Answerer of all,[35]—Anemone,[36]—
Now while thy petals spend the suns about us, hold—
(O Thou whose radiance doth inherit me)[37]
Atlantis,—hold thy floating singer late! [38]

33. Seen lengthwise from a distance, the cordage of the Brooklyn Bridge appears as a pair of pyramids. The "silver sequel" of the pyramids is at one level their luminous progression in space; the phrase may also suggest another alchemical transformation, since silver as well as gold was a goal of alchemical transmutation.

34. The twin pyramids may also appear as a pair of wings, "choiring" because they suggest the flight of singing angels and "white" because (in addition to their electrical illumination and the association of white with angel's wings) they recall the arc of the gull's flight from "To Brooklyn Bridge."

35. An allusion to Whitman's "Song of the Answerer," which celebrates the figure of the poet as a redemptive visionary; note especially the opening and closing statements: "Now list to my morning's romanza, I tell the signs of the Answerer, / To the cities and farms I sing as they spread in the sunshine before me," and "The words of true poems give you more than poems. . . . / Whom they take they take into space to behold the birth of stars, to learn one of the meanings, / To launch off with absolute faith, to sweep through the ceaseless rings and never be quiet again" (ll. 1–2, 82–83).

36. The Bridge as anemone transmutes the "Atlantis rose" of "Cutty Sark." Anemones are a genus of the buttercup family; their petals are broad and curving. Their name, derived from the Greek word for wind, means "windflower"; according to legend, anemones blossom only when brushed by the wind. The flower also has erotic (and homoerotic) associations, based on the classical myth of Venus and Adonis. In the version pertinent here, the blood of the slain Adonis, the beautiful young man adored by the goddess of love, stains the white anemone red. The Bridge undoes the stain and remains inviolate: the "whitest Flower."

37. This sentence literally says that the poet is a legacy bequeathed to the Bridge, which may be glossed to say that, in Hart Crane, the Bridge has found the poet destined to it, passed down from precursors like Whitman. Crane may, however, be inverting the sense of "inherit" to mean "give" rather than "receive" a legacy, in which case it is the Bridge that provides the poet with the heritage destined to him.

38. "Floating singer" remains obscure. One possibility is that Crane is thinking of himself as a descendent of Melville's Ishmael, who survives the shipwreck of the Pequod to become the narrator of *Moby-Dick*. The floating may also recall the conclusion of Coleridge's "Kubla Khan," which predicts a startled response to the sight of the inspired poet: "And all shall cry, Beware! Beware! / His flashing eyes, his floating hair! . . . / For he on honey-dew hath fed / And drunk the milk of Paradise." Another, perhaps closer, match is to a key passage in "The Drunken Boat," by Arthur Rimbaud, whom Crane once called "the last great poet that our civilization will see" (to Waldo Frank, June 20, 1926). The poem is another celebration of visionary poetics; the speaker, afloat on the seas of the world, is the boat of the title: "And from then on I bathed in the Poem / Of the Sea, infused with stars and lactescent, / Devouring the green azure where, like a pale elated / Piece of flotsam, a pensive drowned figure sometimes sinks" (translation by Wallace Fowlie).

So to thine Everpresence, beyond time,
Like spears ensanguined of one tolling star[39]
That bleeds infinity—the orphic strings,[40]
Sidereal phalanxes, leap and converge:
—One Song, one Bridge of Fire![41] Is it Cathay,[42]
Now pity steeps the grass and rainbows ring
The serpent with the eagle in the leaves . . . ?[43]
Whispers antiphonal in azure swing.[44]

39. The conjunction of spears and the "one tolling star" resonates with "The Dance": "And one star, swinging, [took] its place, alone . . . / Until, immortally, it bled into the dawn." The star is the Morning Star, associated in "The Dance" with the dying and reviving Mesoamerican god Quetzalcoatl; at the close of the "The Harbor Dawn" the same star "Turns in the waking west and goes to sleep."

40. The strings of the Bridge are orphic both because they are oracular and because they resemble Orpheus's lyre. Orpheus was one of the Argonauts; he saved them from the Sirens by playing his lyre more beautifully than the Sirens could sing.

41. Having dwelt repeatedly on air, water, and earth, three of the traditional four elements, *The Bridge* in closing merges its myth with the fourth and highest element, fire, a turn anticipated by the gathering "Hand of Fire" at the close of "The Tunnel." The figure is Promethean, uniting technological form with visionary force. But it is also an image of the Bridge illuminated by the rising sun, and in that role it completes the journey toward dawn initiated in "The Tunnel."

42. "Is it Cathay . . .?" echoes and corrects Columbus's boast at the end of the first stanza of "Ave Maria": "I bring you back Cathay!" The echo also points up the fact that "Ave Maria" is composed of octave stanzas that find their justification in the octaves (in every sense) of "Atlantis."

43. The rainbow, the symbol of the divine covenant and, in its arc, a mirror of the curvature of the Bridge, now forms a ring (a circle, symbol of perfection) around the united eagle and serpent, which *The Bridge* explicitly glosses as figures, respectively, of space and time.

44. Antiphony is a pattern of call and response between two musical ensembles, here probably swinging between the two "choiring wings" of the Bridge's span. The ascending motion emphasized throughout "Atlantis" ends in the azure, the blue of the dawn sky. Baudelaire and subsequent French Symbolist poets regularly used azure as a symbol of the ideal; Baudelaire's "The Albatross" calls the great sea birds, and by implication the poets they represent, "kings of the azure." But the Symbolist tradition emphasizes the unknowability and inaccessibility of the *belle Azur*; Crane concludes by literally imagining a bridge—the Bridge—to it.